SCUBA FUNDAMENTAL

Start Diving the Right Way

SIMON PRIDMORE

Sandsmedia Publishing
BALI, INDONESIA

Sandsmedia Publishing, Bali, Indonesia 80363

www.simonpridmore.com

Book Layout ©2016 Createspace.com and Sandsmedia

Cover Image by Andrey Bizyukin

Scuba Fundamental/Simon Pridmore. 1st ed.

ISBN-13: 978-1530524068

ISBN-10: 1530524067

For Mason,
the first of the next generation

The Expert View

"Pitching a book at the correct level for divers-to-be is fraught with difficulty. You have to be honest and engaging but without being scary or overcomplicated. Simon is a great dive writer, and I think he's finally cracked the problem." **Steve Weinmann – Editor, Diver Magazine (UK)**

"Simon's new book, Scuba Fundamental – Start Diving the Right Way, is a thorough, sensible and seriously safety oriented guide for new divers. It is also very, very funny. Simon's anecdotes will make old divers laugh until they cry, whilst promising decades of fun and adventure for new divers. **Judi Lowe, Scuba Instructor, PhD Scholar and Sustainable Dive Tourism Advisor at thedivetourist.**

"I wish I had had this book to read when I learned to dive. I remember being totally confused." **Robin Yao, Executive Editor, EZDIVE magazine**

"This is the book divers should give to friends when they say they want to learn to scuba dive." **Ian Thomas, Author and Scuba Instructor Trainer**

"This is a great book! Simon Pridmore is to be congratulated for this insightful, interesting and honest introduction to scuba diving. He clearly explains the delights of the sport, as well as the potential pitfalls in learning to scuba dive. He tells it as it is! This book will be very valuable, not only for the intending diver, but also for divemasters, instructors and operators as a reminder of how certain things should, and can, be done." **John Lippmann, Founder & Chairman, Divers Alert Network (DAN) Asia-Pacific**

Table of Contents

§1

Before You Begin

1. Start Diving the Right Way

"There's nothing wrong with enjoying looking at the surface of the ocean itself, except that when you finally see what goes on underwater, you realize that you've been missing the whole point of the ocean. Staying on the surface all the time is like going to the circus and staring at the outside of the tent." **Dave Barry, author, columnist and diver.**

Scuba diving is a unique and wonderful sport. It is amazing to be able to spend time beneath the surface of the oceans that cover a huge part of our planet, to see what is down there and watch and interact with the animal life. These are privileges that humans have only enjoyed for the past 70 years or so.

There are few things better in life than a relaxing tour of a coral reef, surrounded by warm clear water, gazing at the incredible variety of the life that exists in our oceans. But that is not all scuba diving can give you. For example, you can cruise around sunken shipwrecks, swim with sea lions, watch manta rays dance, explore underground rivers and visit parts of our planet where comparatively few human beings have ever been.

Nor do you have to be somewhere exotic or do or see something extraordinary to make a dive worthwhile. All over the world, people scuba dive every day just for the sheer fun and camaraderie that the sport offers. A dive club in landlocked Alberta, Canada holds an annual underwater pumpkin carving competition at Thanksgiving each year in a lake. Dozens of local divers turn up. The club reports that last year it was -2C (28F) and snowing sideways and everyone still had a great time.

No matter where you live, there is a good chance that there are folk diving somewhere near you on a regular basis. Often, divers are simply motivated to go diving by the desire to improve their skills. As in any sport, from archery to yoga, the more you do it, the better you get at it.

Why Scuba Fundamental?

Scuba Fundamental is a book for people like you who are thinking of learning to scuba dive. It tells you what you need to know and should do before you sign up for a course. It also gives you impartial and reliable advice on important things about learning to dive that you will not find elsewhere and that most people only discover much later: sometimes too late.

Scuba Fundamental takes you from the germ of the thought that you might like to scuba dive, then continues to guide you to the point where you have completed a couple of courses and twenty or so dives. By that time you will be ready for my book for more advanced divers, Scuba Confidential.

Get Ready and Choose Well

Too many people start learning to scuba dive before they are ready for it. Others are ready but have a poor learning experience when they take the course. In either case, what usually happens next is that they give up the sport, having wasted both time and money, and end up missing out on what could have been a lifetime of incredible experiences. It is not their fault. They just do not know any better.

Before you actually start diving you have no means of judging whether you are properly prepared, physically and psychologically, to dive. Neither do you have any way of distinguishing a good instructor from a bad instructor or a professional dive operator from a cowboy. Anyone can produce a slick website, decorate an attractive looking shop or deliver a persuasive pitch.

The fact is that scuba diving is the same as every other walk of life. There are many wonderful instructors and super-professional dive centres out there. There are also some terrible, lazy and negligent instructors around and operators that deliver poor-quality service and care only about taking your money.

So I decided to write this book to arm you with the knowledge to enable you to make the right decisions about learning to scuba dive. The purpose of Scuba Fundamental is not to teach you how to dive. Your instructor will do that. But Scuba Fundamental will make the process of learning to dive a lot easier for you and help you become a good diver more quickly, avoiding the many pitfalls and wrong turns that lie in wait for the unwary.

Not All Courses Are Equal

If you gather a dozen divers together and turn the conversation to how they learned to dive, you will probably hear a dozen different stories. This is despite the fact that, on paper, the initial scuba diving courses run by the various training agencies are very similar.

Some divers may have done four or five separate swimming pool classes plus four or five separate ocean dives over a number of days before they earned their first diver qualification. Some may only have done as few as two or three water sessions in total, their instructors having combined several required course "dives" into one, in order to save time and money. Others, perhaps older divers, will tell stories of scuba classes that lasted several months and consisted of over twenty water sessions and a dozen dives in the ocean.

The veterans may talk of having had to endure a number of watermanship trials, such as timed swims and snorkelling tests, before they even got their hands on the scuba equipment. By contrast, some of the newer divers may not have even had to show that they could swim before they started the course!

One of the key differences is that, when the older divers learned to dive, they were preparing for a world where there was no mass scuba diving tourism; a world where the fact that you were a qualified scuba diver meant something very different to what it does today. In those days, your qualification meant that you were ready to dive anywhere with another diver of equal ability, under no guided supervision at all. It meant that you had proven your ability to assess a dive site, plan a dive, deal with any contingencies that came your way and rescue yourself or your dive partner in an emergency.

Today, although many scuba diving manuals still promise that your first course will qualify you to dive safely and independently, this is patently not the case. Now, most initial scuba diving classes are much shorter and less intensive than they used to be. You only really have enough time to learn the basics of handling the equipment, managing the equipment in the water and dealing with common problems.

To learn to become a competent, independent diver, as well as a useful and capable partner for another diver, takes more than one quick class and four or five dives. This is why Scuba Fundamental does not just focus on your initial certification course but, instead, accompanies you much further along the path, indicating the route you need to take and giving you the background knowledge you need to make the right choices.

Start diving the right way and you will be relaxed and ready for the adventure. You will have more fun and make fewer mistakes. You will also buy the right equipment at the right time and avoid investing too much too early. I hope you enjoy Scuba Fundamental; that you find it useful, that you discover you love scuba diving and that this is just the start of a life-long passion.

Start diving the right way by

reading Scuba Fundamental.

Scuba Fundamental Jargon Buster

Although I have tried my best to avoid jargon and scuba speak in Scuba Fundamental, especially in the first two sections where I assume the reader has no previous experience of the scuba diving world, I have not always succeeded. Here, therefore, is a brief jargon buster that should help you navigate sections where I introduce new words and concepts.

BCD – an acronym for Buoyancy Compensating Device. This is an inflatable jacket that divers wear to enable them to adjust their buoyancy underwater and on the surface.

Buoyancy – means float-ability. Something that floats on the surface is said to be positively buoyant; something that sinks is negatively buoyant and something that neither rises to the surface nor sinks is neutrally buoyant.

Computer – divers wear a small computer to track depth, time and other aspects of their dives. The computer's primary function is to help the diver avoid decompression illness.

Decompression illness (or the bends) – this is a catch-all term that applies to a variety of problems that can affect divers if they stay at depth too long and ascend too quickly or if they just ascend too quickly at any point in the dive.

Fins – you may know these as "flippers."

Gauges – divers carry gauges as part of their regulator set-up to tell them how deep they are and how much air they have remaining in their cylinder.

Regulator – this is a piece of equipment with a clamp on one end and a mouthpiece on the other end. The regulator is attached to the scuba cylinder and reduces the high pressure air in the cylinder to a pressure that can be breathed by the diver.

Scuba – this is an acronym for Self Contained Underwater Breathing Apparatus. Scuba refers to diving where you take your air supply underwater with you

Submersible Pressure Gauge or SPG – this is the gauge that tells a diver how much air, in units of pressure, they have left in their cylinder.

2. Reasons not to Scuba Dive

Panic in the Shower

A few years ago, a friend who was always saying that she wanted to join one of my beginner's courses called me and told me,

"I woke up this morning and said to myself today's the day I am going to learn to dive."

"Great!" I said.

"The trouble is,' she continued, " I went to have a shower, turned my face up into the spray and immediately started to panic. If I can't even have a shower without freaking out, how can I ever scuba dive?"

I explained that the reason she had panicked was that she had held her breath when she turned her face into the shower and that the human central nervous system is programmed to induce anxiety when a person is not breathing. "On the contrary," I told her, "in scuba diving, you never hold your breath."

I added that this was not to say that she would never become anxious on a scuba dive, but the fact that she had started to panic in the shower was completely irrelevant to the issue of whether she could become a scuba diver.

Eventually she took the course, loved it, as deep down she always knew she would, and is now an enthusiastic diver.

Not for Everyone

You do not have to be a daredevil or a super-fit, well-trained athlete to scuba dive. Scuba divers come from all walks of life and in all shapes and sizes. Some are teenagers, others are great grandparents. Many people count scuba diving among a number of adventure sports they participate in. For many others, diving is the only sport they do.

This is not to say that everyone can scuba dive. Some people cannot dive for medical reasons. They may have physical challenges that mean that they cannot do strenuous exercise. They may have known or undiagnosed cardiovascular disease that may make diving more risky. Or they may not be able safely to breathe air under changing pressure.

They may have psychological issues that mean they should always avoid potentially stressful situations. Scuba diving can involve stress, particularly in the early days, when you are still learning, although one of the main things a scuba class teaches you is how to deal calmly with anything that might happen while you are diving.

Separating the Truth from the Myth

A lot of the reasons that non-divers give for not trying to scuba dive are based on common popular misunderstandings. Many people who would love to learn to scuba dive, like my friend who panicked in the shower, believe it is not for them because they assume either that you need special qualities to scuba dive or that it is dangerous.

Some of these assumptions are false; some are genuine. Some risks do exist: others are cultural myths, figments of the imagination or exaggerated by media hysteria. The aim of this chapter is to separate fact from figment and myth from reality.

First, I would say, that, to quote a Buddhist proverb, "when the student is ready, the master appears." Before you learn to scuba dive, you need to WANT to scuba dive. Whether you are driven by curiosity, spurred by the adventure or simply want to dive in order to share the experience with friends, family or a diving spouse, the will to dive has to come from YOU. Do not learn to dive just because someone else wants you to do it. That sort of scenario often ends in tears.

After you have decided you want to scuba dive, however, doubts may arise. The following are some common concerns.

I want to scuba dive but I can't swim very well.

It seems logical that a diver should be a good swimmer but, strangely, many people do not make the connection. Poor swimmers make poor divers, mainly because they are not comfortable in the water. If you are worried that you may not be able to swim well enough, then invest in some lessons before you start your course. The better you can swim and the happier you are in the water, the easier it will be for you to concentrate on learning to dive and the better a diver you will become. Even if you can swim well, a great way to prepare for a scuba diving course is to spend time before the course doing more swimming to improve your stamina and confidence. I cover this in more detail in the next chapter, "Health and Watermanship."

I want to scuba dive but I can't afford it.

Learning to scuba dive probably costs less than you think it does. Generally speaking, it will cost you less (and take you longer) to learn with a dive club following the schedule they set than to learn with a dive centre that will work to your schedule. However, as I explain in the chapter "Choose Wisely," cost should not be a deciding factor and learning to scuba dive is not something you should look for a bargain basement deal on. If the instructor and dive centre or club you want to learn with charges more for their courses than other places, there is probably a good reason for that. Save up your money to pay for the course you want, rather than go for something cheaper, hoping it will be OK. Before you make the investment, you can see if you like it (and the instructor) by signing up for a scuba experience. This will not cost much and can, in itself, be a life-changing event.

As was the case with a lady named Amanda. This is what she wrote to her first instructor fifteen years after she went scuba diving for the first time.

"I've been meaning to message you for a while. Do you remember myself and 3 friends came to your dive centre in 2001. I was the only one not diving and you took me underwater and spent a very patient sixty minutes with me. Since then I've travelled to some amazing places and seen amazing things diving - most recently thresher sharks in the Philippines. I've done almost 300 dives. I would not have managed any of this without your support and patience that day and I shall be always grateful."

Some dive centres may deduct the cost of the experience from your scuba diving course fee if you sign up afterwards.

You do not have to buy any equipment to use in the course if you do not want to. Use of everything you will need is normally included in the course price. However, as I explain in the chapter "Equipment: Early Purchases," it is actually a very good idea to use some of your own gear when you learn to dive, especially things that will be useful to you when you do other water sports or just spend time on or near the ocean.

I want to scuba dive but I am frightened of sharks.

Thanks mainly to media hysteria and "if it bleeds, it leads" journalism, sharks have an awful and completely undeserved reputation. An instructor who used to teach in Egypt tells the following story.

I had a student once who joined the course, did very well in the pool sessions and passed his theory exam with flying colours. The following day we went to a shallow sandy bay to do his first ocean dive. We were already geared up and ready to get in the water when he asked if there were any sharks in the Red Sea. Thinking that he was excited at the possibility that he might see a shark, I said "yes, but it's unlikely that we'll see one at this site; we never have before."

I added that he would need to do a little more diving and build up some experience before he could go to places elsewhere in the Red Sea where there would be more chance of seeing sharks. He immediately began taking his dive gear off.

"What's happening?" I said.

"I am not going in," he replied.

"Why not?" I asked.

"Because there are sharks here."

"But I told you there aren't any sharks here."

"You said there were sharks in the Red Sea. This is the Red Sea and I am not swimming in the same body of water as a shark!"

And that was that. He cancelled the course and we never saw him again.

The diver's fears were completely without substance. The sharks you see when you scuba dive keep their distance from you and, often, once they have spotted you, they quickly swim off in the other direction. After all, from their perspective you are a strange, noisy, one-eyed bubbling monster and all their instincts tell them to steer clear. A shark attack on a scuba diver is extraordinarily rare. The Washington Post once produced figures that showed that it is much more likely that you will be killed by a cow than a shark!

I understand about sharks but there are other things down there that can hurt me.

There are, and they are often small and difficult to see things that live on the seabed, such as blue-ringed octopus and scorpion fish. But they will not touch you if you do not touch them and one of the golden rules for divers is "don't mess around with the marine life!" One of the primary reasons why so much time in your scuba diving class is taken up with teaching you how to be neutrally buoyant in the water, that is, neither floating nor sinking, is so that you do not come into contact with the seabed, rocks or reefs when you dive. That way, you will not harm the marine life that lives there and it will not harm you.

I want to scuba dive but I am scared of the water.

Fear of water is usually a manifestation of other fears, such as the fear of being unable to control your environment. Swimming classes are the answer. Being able to swim well banishes fears of the water forever. When you can swim well, you are in control in the water. This gives you confidence and you realise that there is no need to be afraid.

I want to scuba dive but it is cold, dark and murky down there.

Of course, most people choose to dive in the tropics where the waters are warm and you can enjoy crystal clear, sunlit seas. But it is a common misconception that the oceans elsewhere are inhospitable to divers. This is not the case. Even in temperate regions, water temperatures average a mild 15C to 20C (60F to 70F) during the diving season and the suits we wear as divers are designed to keep us comfortable for the length of a typical dive and beyond. They are also much easier to get on and off than you might imagine. You will be surprised too at how well you can see and how much there is to see, especially in the comparatively shallow water where most sport diving takes place and where there is still plenty of sunlight penetration.

I want to scuba dive but I am too old.

I have a Brazilian friend who is a retired university professor in his mid-eighties and a keen diver. He recently called me for advice on buying some new equipment. You are probably not too old.

I want to scuba dive but I am scared of getting the bends.

The bends, or decompression illness, is a risk for scuba divers but one of the main purposes of a beginner's course is to show you how to dive in such a way as to minimise the risk. The safe diving procedures you will be taught are well-established and have proven to be very effective at preventing divers from getting the bends.

I want to scuba dive but I don't like to wear anything over my face.

Many people feel like this but your mask is an essential part of your scuba diving equipment. Without it you cannot see very well. It doesn't take long to get used to it. After all it is not that different from wearing big sunglasses. Another advantage of doing a little snorkelling before you embark on scuba diving (see chapter Snorkelling Dos and Don'ts) is that wearing a mask becomes completely routine. If you feel that you may be a little claustrophobic, then choose a mask with a transparent soft silicone skirt that allows plenty of light in and does not make your face feel so "enclosed."

I want to scuba dive but I am afraid my ears will hurt.

One of the first things you will be taught in your scuba diving course is how to make the pressure in your body's air spaces (lungs, ears and sinuses) the same as the surrounding water pressure. This is called equalising and it is usually done by squeezing your nostrils and blowing against your closed nose. You have probably done this before in an aircraft to make your ears pop when you are coming into land and the captain increases the air pressure in the cabin. When you go for the pre-course health check up I recommend in the chapter "Health and Watermanship," one of the main things the doctor will look at and ask you about is the health of your ears. If the doctor clears you for scuba diving, then you have nothing to worry about.

I want to scuba dive but I worry I won't be good at it.

This is actually a good sign. A very healthy attitude to have when embarking on any new activity is a slight fear of failure. It raises your adrenalin, it makes you more attentive and induces you to try harder. A little nervousness is something instructors like to see in their students when they start. It means they are more likely to succeed than people who come to class complacent, thinking they know everything and that it is all going to be easy.

I want to scuba dive but I can't imagine breathing underwater; it's unnatural.

Yes, it is unnatural. We are terrestrial mammals for goodness sake! But you will be amazed how curiously natural it soon feels to breathe underwater. Just a few minutes into your first dive, when you are distracted by all the fish, the feeling of weightlessness, the ability to move around effortlessly in three dimensions and the thrill of entering a whole new world, you will find you are no longer even thinking about it.

Start diving the right way by

knowing that many fears about scuba diving are misplaced.

3. Health and Watermanship

The young couple walked into the dive centre hand in hand and announced that they were on their honeymoon and wanted to learn to scuba dive together. They seemed very excited. Andrina, their instructor, sat down with them and took them through the schedule, explaining that there was a little paperwork to complete before they got on with the course. This included a health declaration.

She left them alone for a couple of minutes, but when she returned the girl stood up and approached her. She indicated a point half way down the health declaration, where it asked, "Are you or could you be pregnant?" She whispered "do I have to be truthful?" Andrina nodded, "yes." "And, if I might be pregnant, I can't dive?" Andrina shook her head, "no, I'm afraid not. The pressure changes your body is subjected to while you are diving may harm the baby." The girl looked crestfallen, "I had no idea; if only I had known…" Her voice trailed away as she had a sudden thought. She cocked her head in the direction of her new husband. "He doesn't know yet!"

Andrina said she was going for a walk along the beach and would be back in ten minutes. When she returned the couple hardly noticed, so engrossed were they in each other. They apologised for taking up her time but, in the circumstances, they would not be learning to dive on this holiday. Andrina wished them every happiness.

The first time most prospective divers are exposed to the medical issues involved with scuba diving is on day one of their course, when they are given a health declaration to review and complete. Among other things, this form contains a list of things that might preclude someone from scuba diving safely. As Andrina's student discovered, one of these things is pregnancy.

Bad Timing

The actual day they begin their scuba course is not the best time for people to find out that they have a health background that suggests it would be wise for them to consult a doctor before proceeding any further. They have already made the decision, committed themselves to the class and have turned up excited at the prospect of going scuba diving. Their instructors are prepared too. They are also conscious of how much they have to get through in a limited amount of time. So they are eager to get the paperwork out of the way and get started.

Andrina's students had much more important things on their minds after learning that they would have to postpone their diving plans. But for most people there is no upside to the suggestion that they may not be able to do the course on medical grounds. Therefore, when student divers see an issue on the health declaration that they think may apply to them, they can be inclined to check "no" when they should check "yes," or vice versa. Or they ask their instructors for advice. Now, most instructors have no medical knowledge at all beyond basic first aid and it would be extremely unusual if they had any acquaintance at all with the medical history of their students. So their response to any question of this nature should be to tell the student to talk to a doctor before proceeding with the class. But they are often reluctant to do this, as they do not want anyone to drop out of the course. So they will often connive with the student to check whichever response allows them all to carry on.

This is obviously a practice that puts both students and instructors at risk. For the students the risk is to their safety. For the instructors, the risk is one of legal exposure that could threaten their career. The students rationalise the risk, thinking that the instructors are professionals, they must know what they are doing and they would never accept someone on the course if they thought they were not fit to dive. The instructors' rationale is that, if the students really had a significant health issue, they would not have signed up for the course in the first place. Some may even be thinking. "let's see how it goes." This, of course, is completely irresponsible on their part.

Get a Check Up

Evidently, you should not leave the decision on whether you are medically fit to dive to a dive instructor. To make sure you turn up on day one of your course ready to go, arrange a health check up well in advance of the course. Ideally, go to see a diving doctor, that is, a physician who is familiar and up-to-date with diving medicine. Most general practitioners have no training in, and little understanding of, diving medicine and that is why I specify a diving doctor. I also say up-to-date because, as in all fields of medicine, current wisdom changes as new research studies emerge or new treatments become available. For example, in the past, if you had asthma or diabetes, no doctor would ever clear you for scuba diving. Now, even if you have either condition, as long as it is carefully monitored, under control and you are able to do exercise, there is a good chance that you can scuba dive.

Getting a full heath check before you start a diving course is especially important if, as many people do, you are coming into the sport later in life, perhaps after your children have left home and you have more free time and disposable income. Scuba diving can be strenuous and both physiologically and physically demanding.

Even if you are younger, a health check is still a good idea, just to make sure you have no issues that may be exacerbated by scuba diving. It may well be that you are fit and engage in a variety of sports already without any problem, but that does not necessarily mean you are fit to dive. Scuba diving is different primarily because, a) you are underwater and b) you are breathing compressed air.

Ailments that are not life threatening at all on land can become a problem when you are diving, where loss of consciousness or loss of self-control, because of a seizure perhaps, can lead you to drown. Similarly, if you have a history of bronchial, sinus or ear problems, this could mean that scuba diving is not for you. This is because the pressure of the air in your body's airspaces changes frequently when you dive and obstruction of the airways may cause permanent damage and can even be life-threatening.

Children

Children are a special case and the issue of what age they are able to learn to scuba dive is more complex than you might think. Scuba diver training agencies tend to have a one-size-fits-all attitude towards this, stating that at one age children can do this and, at another age, they can do that. This sort of approach is not appropriate where children are concerned. Children develop physically, psychologically and socially at different speeds. Consider the difficult issues faced by schools and teachers when children of the same age exhibit vastly different levels of physical prowess, maturity and understanding.

So just because a training agency says that children of 12 can learn to scuba dive as long as they have parental consent, this does not mean that your 12-year-old child should do a diving course. Nor is there any point consulting your local dive centre. Dive professionals have no expertise at all in assessing whether a child is ready to scuba dive. Nor do they receive any specific training in teaching children to dive. They are certainly no more able to judge your child's suitability than you are. In fact, they are much less able. You know your own child; they do not.

The question of when a child can learn to scuba dive should be managed on a case-by-case basis, taking into account educational, physical, physiological, psychological and equipment factors, as well as basic issues such as their swimming ability, comfort in the water and the availability of an instructor you trust. Reading, comprehension and communication skills are important too.

I have three children, all girls, all wonderful, vibrant, inspiring people. But they are also very different people. They spent much of their childhood on the water, in the water and hanging around with divers. When each of them asked me to teach them to dive, the situational circumstances were ideal. I trusted myself as an instructor and was free to supervise any and all diving they did, either as part of the class or afterwards. I owned a dive centre that stocked equipment sized for small children, such as tiny cylinders and BCDs. We even had child-sized snorkel and regulator mouthpieces. All three girls had been swimming almost as long as they had been walking and were as comfortable in the water as fish. Finally, I had a close friend, a specialist in diving medicine, who had been the girls' doctor for a number of years.

I taught my eldest girl to dive at the age of 12. She was strong enough to carry the equipment. She was very sensible, listened well, processed information intelligently and was a precocious reader. She also had a close friend who was a couple of years older and who wanted to learn to dive too and I thought they would make a good team. I feel that it is very important that children are taught to dive separately from adults and in very small groups to maximise instructor contact time and ensure they have the close attention they need.

When my second daughter reached the age of 12, she had a smaller frame than her sister. She also had a vivid imagination, tended to daydream and could be impulsive. I decided to wait until she was stronger and more emotionally mature before I taught her to dive, so she had to wait until she was nearly 15.

When my third daughter was 12 she was diagnosed with a condition, common in children, known as patent foramen ovale (PFO), a small opening between the right and left atria of the heart. By the time most people become adult, the opening has closed but research suggests that a PFO remains present in 10 to 20% of adults. Studies indicate, however, that around

50% of divers who experience unexplained decompression sickness have a PFO.

To date, research papers have stopped short of concluding that people who have a PFO should not dive. Nor are divers who are diagnosed with a PFO advised necessarily to have an operation to close it before they go diving again as, like any surgery, the operation carries its own risks. But divers with a PFO are encouraged to take greater precautions against decompression sickness when they dive, such as spending less time at depth and ascending even more slowly than usual.

In my daughter's case, she decided that scuba diving was not that important to her and she was happy just to swim and snorkel when she went out on boat trips. The plan was to check when she became an adult to see if the PFO had closed naturally and then think again about scuba diving, but, by that time, her life revolved around hobbies and sports completely unrelated to the sea so the question did not arise. And it was certainly not my place to insist.

It is important to remember that, just because you, the parents, may be divers, this does not mean that your children will automatically be ready and willing to follow in your finsteps as soon as they can. Also, when your children reach "I want to dive" age, consider all the factors I mention here and read online the opinions of doctors and educators much more knowledgeable than I am.

If you are in any doubt regarding your circumstances or location, the facilities and equipment available, strength issues, medical issues, emotional maturity issues, learning issues or anything else, just wait. There is no hurry. In the meantime, your children can still swim, snorkel and duck dive to their hearts' content.

Watermanship

Before you learn to scuba dive, you have to be able to swim. The main reason for this is that the equipment you use as a diver can fail and your survival can depend on your ability to swim and float without any equipment to assist you.

Most beginner's courses require you to be able to swim, wearing a bathing suit and nothing else, for around 200m (650ft) without stopping or touching the bottom (or the side of a pool, or a boat, or anything else.) You must also be able to float or tread water at the surface unaided for ten minutes.

You should be asked to demonstrate to your instructor before the course begins that you can complete these tasks. An instructor who does not ask you to perform the swim tests is not doing you a favour. Your safety and survival are at stake. The swim test requirements represent the minimum level of watermanship that a new diver should have. If you struggle to achieve them then you are not ready to start scuba diving. Fear of water and over-dependence on your scuba equipment are common pre-cursors to panic and panic kills more scuba divers than anything else.

If you have any fears of the water, confront and overcome these BEFORE you begin a scuba diving course. You may have assumed that swimming lessons are included in the course. They are not. Take swimming lessons with a qualified teacher to improve your style and strength. Learn different strokes and, in particular, develop your leg strength. Practise swimming without goggles or a mask and with your face in the water in between breaths. If you are in a heavily chlorinated pool, close your eyes as you swim as the chlorine will sting. In the sea or in a natural pool, swim with your eyes open.

Once you are accustomed to the feeling of water on your face, go one step further. Stand in shallow water, take a breath and, holding onto the side of the pool, squat down until your head is below the surface. Do this for a few seconds only at first, then extend the time you stay under water. Get used to the sensation of being completely immersed. Trust me, however unlikely this may sound now, you will come to love it.

Finally, practise swimming under water in the sea holding your breath with your eyes open. Once you can do this you are ready to snorkel, which is an essential preparatory skill that every potential scuba diver should acquire, as I describe in the next chapter.

Start diving the right way by

making sure there are no medical issues that will prevent you from diving, and

getting into the swim of things.

4. Snorkelling Dos and Don'ts

If you are thinking of scuba diving and have never snorkelled before: hold it right there. Postpone that scuba class you were planning to take. Not only is snorkelling a great pastime on its own, it is also the perfect way to prepare for scuba diving. You use much of the same equipment, many of the techniques are similar and snorkelling will increase your comfort in the water immensely.

Go on holiday, pick a resort that offers snorkelling on site and snorkel from the beach. Or join a dive boat as a snorkeler. Check first that they are going to a site with a shallow reef where you can snorkel to your heart's content while the divers do their thing a little deeper down.

Hanging out with divers will also give you a real insight into what scuba diving is like and help you decide whether it is for you. The divers will no doubt ask when you are going to take a scuba course, to which you can simply answer, "later. For now, I am enjoying being a snorkeler."

Don't let them get away with implying that somehow snorkelers are lesser beings than divers. You may even see more interesting things than they do! The sea turtle that hears those noisy bubbling things approaching and swims away to avoid them will often come right by you as you lie still and silent on the surface.

The top is always the most colourful part of a coral reef because sunlight illuminates the shallows much better than the depths and the shallows are home to a huge variety of marine life. Divers typically spend only a small part of each dive in shallow water. They would do well to spend more time there, especially in the middle of a sunny day, when it can be truly glorious.

Tips and Tricks

Here are a few tips on how to get the most out of snorkelling. I cover the techniques here in greater detail than I cover scuba diving techniques later in Scuba Fundamental. I do this for a good reason. When you learn to dive, your instructor will spend a lot of time working with you on your scuba skills. On the other hand, it is rare that a dive centre will offer you instruction on how to snorkel. They will usually just rent you the equipment, point the way to the reef and leave you to figure it out on your own.

But, as with any activity, if you are armed with a few ideas from the start and can avoid most of the pitfalls, your learning curve will be much less steep and you will enjoy it more. Later, you will be able to apply all these techniques to scuba diving too.

What to Wear

Cover up when you snorkel in tropical regions as the sun striking your body via a thin layer of salt water can burn even tanned skin. Snorkel wearing a minimum of tee shirt and shorts, but be aware that this will still leave your arms and calves exposed. If you use sunscreen, make sure it does not contain chemicals that can harm the reef when the screen washes off your body. Check before buying. If a sunscreen is reef-friendly, it will say so on the bottle.

It is far better to wear a full length Lycra dive skin. This will also come in useful when you subsequently start to scuba dive, as you can wear it under your neoprene wetsuit as additional thermal protection. Wearing a dive skin under your wetsuit also makes it easier to get the wetsuit on and off.

If you feel cold in the water just with a dive skin, then of course you can snorkel wearing a neoprene wetsuit too. The main problem with doing this is that neoprene suits are buoyant. The thicker they are, the more thermal protection they provide but also the more buoyant they are. This additional positive buoyancy makes it more difficult for you to duck dive, (see below.) However, if you are not yet a completely confident swimmer, then the positive buoyancy of a neoprene wetsuit helping to keep you afloat at the surface will make you feel more comfortable in the water.

Scuba divers wear lead weights to counteract the positive buoyancy of their wetsuit and help them descend below the surface. As a snorkeler, you should never wear weights. If someone proposes these as a solution to help you to duck dive while wearing a neoprene wetsuit, politely refuse. Duck diving is a great thing to do but it is not essential to a satisfying snorkelling experience. It is much more important that you are comfortable on the surface and don't have to expend effort and energy just to stay afloat. The last thing you want to be burdened with are objects whose sole function is to make you sink. If you can't duck dive in your wetsuit, so be it. Just enjoy the view from above.

Wear reef shoes or dive boots. Beaches do not only consist of soft, powdery sand. They can be strewn with rocks, stones and razor sharp bits of coral. Also, as you are strolling into the water through the shallows, there may be obstacles such as small boulders hidden below the surface. So you need to protect your feet.

This means that the fins you should use are the open-heeled style that you can wear with shoes and boots. In the next chapter "Equipment – Early Purchases," I discuss choosing fins in more detail.

Time and Place

First and foremost, choose the right time and place to snorkel. Pick a place where the reef or rocks are close to the surface and where there is no boat or Jet Ski traffic. Many beaches have snorkelling areas that are cordoned off.

 Choose a time of day when the water is calm and clear and there is only minimal wave action. If the ocean is rough, cancel your snorkelling plans. It will be a miserable experience and getting in and out of the water can be difficult: as Jeff, an experienced diver who should have known better, discovered.

"A while ago, I took my 12-year-old nephew snorkeling for the first time. Well, that was the idea anyway."

"We drove down to Marmion Marine Park where there is a shallow reef just offshore. It was windy and there were waves breaking. My initial thought was to cancel the plan but I was so keen to give him the experience of a lifetime that I allowed my enthusiasm to out-vote my caution. I held on to him as we stepped bravely into the surf zone. I was in such a hurry to get behind the waves that I ran right into some rocks, broke a toe and gashed my leg open."

"I soldiered on. My nephew had difficulty getting his fins on, even though I was holding onto him. He was nervous and kept taking his snorkel out of his mouth, which of course allowed water to flood in and make him choke. It was at that point that I thought, "enough!" "

"I limped out of the water nursing my sore toe and with blood running down my leg. Later that afternoon, my nephew got his revenge for my nearly drowning him. I had dozed off, exhausted from the morning's exertions. Disappointed that his Uncle Jeff was not entertaining him, my nephew decided to make his own entertainment and sprayed my open leg wound with antiseptic. That opened my eyes so quickly that I bruised my eyelids."

Preparation

Before you start, clean your mask so that it doesn't fog up while you are in the water. When the glass is still dry, spit in it or use a commercial defogging liquid. Baby shampoo works really well too. Wipe the spit/ defog liquid / baby shampoo around the inside of the mask with your finger.

Make sure that your finger is clean and dry first. A mistake many people make is to apply sunscreen before they clean their mask and just end up covering the lens in oily residue. This almost guarantees that the mask will fog up once you put it on.

Then rinse the spit/defog/baby shampoo out in fresh or salt water. Don't touch the glass as or after you rinse it. The product you applied to the glass acts as a surfactant to stop fog forming. If you touch the glass after the surfactant is applied, you risk removing it.

Bring a Friend

Don't snorkel alone. Snorkelling is hardly a high-risk activity but it is always a good idea to snorkel with someone else or as part of a loose group. After all, the ocean is an environment with which you are not completely familiar. Although your snorkelling partners may be no more experienced than you, multiple sets of senses might detect trouble coming before one set of senses. It is also reassuring to have a companion around in case something goes wrong. If you have cramp or are stung by a jellyfish, having someone to help you get back to shore turns a potentially serious emergency into just a minor inconvenience.

From the Beach

Enter the water with your mask and snorkel around your neck and the heel straps of your fins looped over one forearm. Never walk wearing fins. You will fall over. If you feel that, despite this wise advice, you nevertheless have to walk in to the water wearing fins, then walk in backwards.

You carry your equipment as I described so that you have one free arm to balance yourself as you walk into the sea. It also makes sure you won't lose anything if a wave catches you or you trip on a rock and fall over. Wait until you are beyond the wave line before you address the issue of getting your fins on. Bend your knees so most of your body is immersed and supported by the water. Then put your fins on, one by one. Use your snorkelling partner for support and cross one leg over the other to pull each fin on by the strap. Tighten the straps so that your feet are held securely in the fin pockets. Then help your snorkelling partner do the same.

Once you have both fins on, stand up straight and put your mask and snorkel in place. Your mask should feel comfortable. Don't pull the strap too tight. If you find that water comes in while you are wearing it, don't tighten it even further. Instead, counter-intuitively perhaps, loosen it a little so that the flexible silicone skirt can mould itself to the contours of your face. Leave your mask in place all the time when you are in the water. Not only does your mask help you see the marine life below, it stops water from going up your nose. Don't ever push it up on to your forehead. If you do that, more often than not, the next thing that will happen is that you get a wave in the face and sea water up your nose.

It does not matter which side of your face you wear your snorkel on. Divers usually keep their snorkel on the left side of the mask as the scuba regulator they breathe from when they dive comes over their right shoulder and they don't want to get their snorkel caught up in the regulator hose. Try doing it this way first. If you don't like it for some reason, switch it to the right side next time you snorkel.

Look down as you swim rather then ahead. If you raise your head to look forward, your snorkel can tilt back below the surface and give you a mouthful of seawater rather than fresh air when you next try to breathe from it. If your snorkel does fill up with water, blow it out forcefully. If you have no air in your lungs, first turn your face away from any wave action. Then take the snorkel out of your mouth, take a deep breath in, put the snorkel back in and exhale strongly to clear it.

To leave the water, approach the beach then turn and face out to sea before standing up, so you can watch for any waves heading your way. Slip your mask and snorkel down around your neck. Watch the waves, wait for a calm patch of water, then bend your knees and remove your fins as before, holding on to your snorkelling partner as you do so. Loop the fin straps over your forearm again and head for the beach through the wave zone.

From a Boat

Most of the ways you would enter the water from a boat as a snorkeler are identical to the techniques scuba divers use. Getting used to making the entries in just a mask, snorkel and fins is great practice for doing them later in your dive class wearing all the extra scuba equipment.

"Giant Stride" Entry

Put your suit, boots, mask, snorkel and fins on while you are sitting on the boat. When you are ready, shuffle to the entry platform and look around to make sure the entry zone is clear of people or obstacles. Then put one hand flat on your face, with your palm on the snorkel mouthpiece and fingers splayed on the front of your mask to hold it in place. Rest the other hand on your stomach rather than waving it around. Look straight out to the horizon, take a deep breath in, hold it, then make a confident, big step forward with one leg. This is your "giant stride." Don't hop. Believe me, the other leg will follow you without you having to worry about it.

If you have executed the "giant stride" correctly, you will enter the water vertically and your head will hardly go below the surface at all. Even if your impetus does carry you down, because you took a deep breath before you stepped out, you will pop back up immediately. Don't make the common mistake of looking down at the water as you step bravely out. If you look down, the first thing to hit the water will be your face and, despite the fact that you are holding on to it, the impact will probably make your mask fly off.

Back Roll Entry

If the boat has no entry platform, you will usually sit on the side and roll into the water backwards. Again, put everything on first. Then sit on the side of the boat, facing inwards, with your legs tucked up beneath you. Look behind you to make sure the area is completely clear. If there is nothing in your way, turn back, look straight ahead across the boat and hold your mask and snorkel as you did when you made the "giant stride" entry. Take a deep breath in, hold it and roll backwards into the water. When you come back up to the surface, as you will almost immediately, exhale to clear the water out of your snorkel and kick away from the boat.

Getting Back In the Boat

Usually the boat will have a ladder to help you get back in. Swim to the ladder and hold it while you remove your fins, one by one, and hand them up to the crew or place them on the deck. Don't remove your fins before you have a tight hold of the ladder just in case the boat floats away and you have to chase it a little. Neither should you take your mask and snorkel off before your fins because you may need to look underwater to see where the fin buckles and straps are. This is all new to you, after all. If the boat has no ladder, then you will need to get back in by pulling yourself up and over the side. Don't take your fins off before you do this. Keeping them on and kicking as you pull yourself up will make getting back into the boat much easier.

Take your mask and snorkel off once you are back in the boat and put them away directly into your bag or boat box. Don't leave them lying around. They are light and easily knocked off the side of a boat.

How to Duck Dive

Duck diving allows you to get a closer look at the marine life on the reef and also allows you to experience, albeit briefly, the freedom of being able to move through the water in three dimensions, up, down and laterally. It is the closest you can get to swimming like a fish, or like a scuba diver.

This is how you do it. Lie facedown on the surface. Take a breath. Hold the breath, then duck your head underwater, bending at the waist to make yourself as vertical as possible. Throw your legs straight up into the air, so that their weight carries your upper body down under the water. Then make one breaststroke pull with your arms to bring you down further. Your legs and fins will now be completely below the surface so you can start kicking yourself down towards the seabed.

You will feel pressure on your ears as you descend, as the water pressure is greater than the air pressure in your body air spaces. With forefinger and thumb, hold your nostrils together through your mask's flexible nosepiece and try to blow gently against your blocked nose. This is the process called equalising that I mentioned in Chapter 2. You should feel your ears pop. If they don't pop, they will hurt, at which point stop descending and go back up to the surface.

If they do pop, then keep finning down. Don't pull any more with your arms, just fin with a long scissor kick, (see below.) When you get near the bottom, straighten out to a horizontal profile and look around. When you feel the urge to breathe, head back to the surface, looking up as you do so, to make sure you don't bump into a boat or another snorkeler.

While you are underwater, keep your snorkel clenched between your teeth and hold your breath. When you reach the surface nod your head forward so you are looking downwards. The end of your snorkel will now be up in the air. Exhale forcefully into the snorkel to clear it of water. Then take a fresh breath, inhaling cautiously, just in case there is residual water in the snorkel, and keep swimming.

A couple of caveats: first, before duck-diving, don't hyper ventilate, that is, don't take a series of fast, shallow breaths to try to give yourself more time underwater. This is dangerous. Second, the rule for duck diving with your snorkelling partner is "one up, one down." One of you should always remain on the surface watching while the other dives.

How to Swim

When you snorkel, you very rarely use your hands or arms. You mostly use your fins for propulsion and to change direction. Keep your arms by your side or folded across your chest. While you are lying on the surface watching the marine life below, just keep your legs and fins still and stretched out on the surface behind you.

If you want to move, then use your fins. To move slowly, keep your legs stretched out behind you and flutter your fins like paddles on the surface. To swim a little more quickly, you can use a frog kick like a breaststroke swimmer, which generates greater power. You move your legs apart slowly then bring your fins together to give you forward propulsion.

If you want to move fast, then you use the classic wide, powerful scissor kick that scuba divers use to counter a current. This kick is a long stroke with your legs straight but slightly bent at the knees, using your thigh muscles for power and deploying the whole face of the fin to push the water down and behind you, so that you move forwards. It takes a lot of energy and strength to sustain this sort of kick for long, which is why many scuba divers favour the frog kick instead.

What you absolutely must not do is move your fins with your legs bent, shuffling your knees back and forward underneath you frantically; the way a dog moves when it paddles. This creates no forward movement at all and you just expend energy for no purpose. Also, because your legs and fins drop below you when you try to swim this way, you usually end up kicking the reef and damaging marine life, as well as yourself. When you snorkel, you and your fins should always be on the surface, except when you go underwater completely on a duck dive.

Learning to use your fins in a variety of ways is an important step towards becoming a good scuba diver. Practising the techniques, developing the skills and building finning habits before you even start your scuba class puts you well ahead of the game.

Things to be Wary Of

Stingers

Many reefs are covered with hydroids. These are animals that look like pretty ferns. They are covered in stinging cells called nematocysts so avoid touching them if you duck dive down to take a closer look at the reef. They will not cause you any lasting damage if you brush against them but the rash will itch for a couple of days. Sometimes as you swim you will feel little pinpricks against your exposed skin. Don't worry, these are almost invisible, free-floating nematocysts that just cause temporary discomfort and leave no marks. If you wear a full length dive skin, you will only feel them occasionally against your cheeks and hands. This is another good reason to keep covered up.

Currents

If you are ever snorkelling and find that you are still moving even when you are not finning or that, when you fin, you seem to be going unusually fast, the chances are that you have been caught in a current, a river of moving water in the ocean. If you are snorkelling from a beach, the current will usually take you parallel to the shore. If this happens, don't fight the current and try to swim back to your starting point. You will only tire yourself out. Instead head straight for the shore and walk back.

If you are snorkelling from a boat, again don't try and compete in a trial of strength with the ocean. You will not win. Instead, signal the boat by waving your arms or waving a fin in the air and get the boat to come and pick you up.

Beware of rip currents. These are caused when water flows over the top of a reef towards the shore and then flows back out to sea through a gap in the reef. This gap can seem to be a good way for a snorkeler to get out to the back of the reef. The problem is that, although it may be easy to swim out of the gap following the direction in which the water is moving, it will be impossible to get back via the same route, against the flow.

Many swimmers have come to harm, either because they exhaust themselves fighting the rip current or injure themselves trying to climb over the reef when they get into difficulty. Never swim out through a gap in a reef when water is breaking over the top.

Start diving the right way by

doing plenty of snorkelling first.

5. Equipment: Early Purchases

You don't absolutely need to bring anything other than a swimsuit when you turn up for your first scuba diving class. You can usually borrow everything else you need from the dive centre or dive club that is running the course.

However, I strongly suggest you DO buy some of the equipment before you start, rather than borrowing. In the previous two chapters "Health and Watermanship" and "Snorkelling Dos and Don'ts," I talked about what a good idea it is to prepare for scuba diving long before you actually start the class, by spending time in the water, improving your swimming skills and doing plenty of snorkelling.

You will be much more comfortable swimming and snorkelling with good quality equipment that you have chosen yourself: things you like, that fit well and make you look good.

Don't Buy Everything

I am not recommending that you buy all your scuba gear before you do your first class. After all, you may find you don't like scuba diving or don't have time for it. Not all people who learn to scuba dive end up becoming lifetime divers and this is usually not because they don't like the sport. It is just that other factors intrude on diving plans; factors such as children, work, financial issues or other hobbies and lifestyle choices.

The things that I advise you to buy before the course will not only make you more comfortable while you are preparing and practising, they will also help you make the transition to scuba diving more easily, because when you start the class you will be using and wearing equipment that you are already accustomed to. Good quality equipment will also serve you well for many scuba diving years ahead. If you do subsequently decide that for some reason scuba diving is not for you, then you can still use everything I talk about in this chapter for snorkelling, doing other water sports or just when you spend time at the beach.

Let me illustrate the point with a culinary metaphor. Say you are very interested in food and want to train to be a chef. You sign up for classes and buy a good set of kitchen knives. Later, you decide you don't want to embark on a career in cooking but your knives are still a good investment because you now have excellent tools to use for cooking at home.

The Perils of Borrowed Gear

The alternative to buying is to borrow or rent things that have been used and abused by a hundred people before you. It is not uncommon to encounter dive centres that lend out old and sub-standard equipment to new divers. Their argument is that they don't want to waste money on giving them good equipment to use, because they will not appreciate it and, besides, they are not experienced enough to know the difference. This is not a valid argument. Wearing a wetsuit that is old, thin and does not fit you or using equipment that is mouldy, damaged or broken makes learning to dive more difficult than it should be. The discomfort of using bad gear could even persuade you not to continue with the sport.

The life support items that you borrow from the dive centre, your regulator, BCD, gauges and computer, will usually work just fine. After all, nobody wants you to come to harm during the class.

It is the basic equipment that it is usually in poor condition. I once consulted for a hotel chain that was interviewing companies to run the dive centre in their new resort. One applicant, a very well known operation with many branches, invited me and one of the resort directors to go diving with their flagship dive centre in order to impress us. The owner of the company himself took us out.

The hotel director, a new diver, did not have his own equipment. "No problem," the owner said, "you can use ours." All the equipment was pretty shabby but it was the fins that were the real attention-grabbers. There was a thick white wear line where the foot pocket joined the blade and you could easily bend the blades up and down beyond 180 degrees. In the water the fins just flapped around uselessly on the end of the diver's feet, giving him no means of propulsion at all. When we pointed this out, the owner shrugged his shoulders and blamed previous customers for breaking the fins. He said he would offer to give the director another pair but these were the best he had available. Needless to say, his company did not get the contract.

When you learn to dive and borrow the dive centre's equipment, look at what your instructors are wearing and compare it to what you have been given to use. Yours should at least look similar to theirs. If it looks substantially inferior, don't just accept it; ask "Why?"

Where to Buy

Don't buy your dive clothing or equipment in a supermarket or discount warehouse. Buy it from a specialist dive shop or sports store, where you have the benefit of advice from sales people who know what they are talking about. Buying online is an option and although, in the past, it might have been difficult to shop on the Internet for things that need to fit you, today's online retailers are much more sophisticated and offer detailed size charts and live consultation. Many also offer no-questions-asked refunds if you are not satisfied. The most important thing is to have expert advice, whether you get it from someone standing in front of you or someone chatting to you on your screen.

When you introduce yourself to the sales staff, point out that you are looking for equipment because you plan to do a scuba diving course at some point in the future but that you will use it to do some snorkelling first. Tell the staff that you want the quality of equipment that experienced divers use, because you plan to use it for several years. Then look at the range of products presented and shop according to your budget.

Suited and Booted

In the chapter "Snorkelling Dos and Don'ts," I mentioned the advantages of buying a full-length dive skin and, if you are swimming in cooler waters, a neoprene wetsuit. I suggested also that you should buy a pair of reef shoes or dive boots.

As with everything you buy, try it on first, take your time to choose and don't accept any compromise on fit or comfort. A well-fitting wetsuit can be difficult to find. The suits are made in a limited range of sizes and shapes and people tend to come in a far wider range of configurations. If you are female, look for suits designed for female bodies. Beware of the ladies' lines peddled by some manufacturers, which are just suits for men, but in pastel shades.

The suit should reach your wrists and ankles without bunching on the legs or arms. It should not bunch on the torso either. If it does, this means it is too large. Bunching is bad because it does not allow the wetsuit to perform its major function, which is to allow a thin layer of water in next to your skin. Your skin warms this layer of water and this helps to insulate you from the cooler water around you. If water can move in and out and through the suit, then the suit is useless.

Neither should a neoprene suit be so tight that you find it constricting when you zip it up. If you find it impossible to find a suit that fits you "off the peg" then you can have one custom-made. This is not as expensive as you might think.

In very cold climates, divers wear something called a drysuit. This looks and functions like an astronaut's space suit, minus the helmet. A drysuit is expensive and definitely does not fit into the category of equipment you would use anyway even if you do not continue with scuba diving. So, if you are planning to learn to dive in waters where drysuits are commonly used, borrow or rent one, rather than buying.

Masks, Snorkels and Fins

I mentioned in the previous chapter that, as you will be wearing reef shoes or dive boots, the style of fin you will need is one with an open heel pocket that you can slip your booted foot into. You secure your foot in the pocket by tightening the heel strap. In dive stores, you will also find closed or full-foot fins, which you wear with bare feet or thin fin socks, but people generally only use these when they dive exclusively from boats.

There are a vast variety of styles and models of open-heeled fin on the market and you will be amazed at how much technology goes into the creation of what is really just a simple foot extension device that allows you to displace more water with each kick and therefore move faster.

The companies that make the fins that the vast majority of divers use are Tusa, Cressi Sub and Mares. There will definitely be dive centres near you that stock one or more of these brands. None of these companies make a bad fin. In the unlikely event that you cannot find a stockist, you would not go wrong either if you chose any model sold by Aqualung, US Divers or Oceanic. I am not paid to promote these brands. This is just how it is.

At this stage, there is no point getting bogged down in the finer points of fin design. Buy a fin with a simple heel strap as all straps will break one day and the more complex straps are more expensive to replace. Buy a fin with a single solid blade. If you have very strong leg muscles, buy a fin with a stiff blade. Otherwise, buy a model that has flexible panels that allow the blade to curve a little when you kick against the water. Then choose according to your budget. There are models on the market with split blades or with convoluted planes and angles that would not look out of place on a superhero costume. Ignore them for now. Make sure you buy your reef shoes or dive boots before you buy your fins so you can wear them when you try your fins on.

You can be equally blinded by technology when choosing a snorkel or mask. Again, as with the fins, keep it simple. Choose from the brands I mentioned earlier. Go for a snorkel that has a one way purge valve at the bottom to make it easier to clear it and some sort of protection at the top of the tube to minimize water entry on the surface.

When choosing a mask, ignore the models with large single panes of glass and side windows. They might offer you wider vision underwater but their internal volume makes it more difficult to clear them with one breath. Choose a standard, twin-lens, low-volume mask with a soft skirt that will mould easily to the contours of your face. Try on a variety of masks to compare the fit. An oft-quoted piece of advice is to put the mask on, inhale through your nose and see if it sticks. Well, I can tell you now, pretty much any mask will stick to your face if you do that, whether it fits well or not.

The best way to make sure a mask fits is to take it in the water and good dive centres will have samples that you can try in their pool. If that option is not available, then try each mask on with a snorkel in your mouth, press the mask lightly to your face and a), make sure the nosepiece doesn't touch the bridge of your nose, and b), run your fingers around the skirt to make sure there are no gaps. You do this with the snorkel fitted because, when you purse your lips to encompass the snorkel's mouthpiece, this tends to accentuate the smile channels between your nose and cheeks. If the mask is too small or the skirt is not sufficiently flexible, then you will find gaps there that water will be able to seep in through.

New Mask Syndrome

This advice will also be in your first scuba diving manual but I mention it here as you probably will not have reached that stage yet. New masks have a silicone film on the inside of the glass and you need to remove this or your mask will fog up as soon as you put it on. Toothpaste works well and leaves your mask smelling nice and minty. Use the regular white toothpaste rather than gel, as it needs to be gently abrasive. Squeeze a glob of toothpaste out then rub it around the dry glass, inside and out, before flushing all the paste away with water. Then dry the glass and repeat the exercise four or five times, depending on how effective your rubbing has been! You will only know if you have been successful when you try the mask on. Spend time on this. It is extremely irritating to have a mask that fogs up all the time. Although you are taught in your scuba class how to deal with a misty mask, it spoils your dive if you find you have to do it every couple of minutes.

Although you may have prepared the mask well when you bought it, you still need to clean it beforehand each time you use it, as I described in the previous chapter.

Bags

Finally, you will need to buy some bags. Get a string bag, large enough to hold your mask, fins, snorkel, boots and suit. This will enable you to keep all your equipment together and tidily stowed away when you go snorkelling or diving. Dive boats are busy places and you need to be organised. See the chapter "Aspects of Etiquette" later for more on this. Also, buy a dry bag to keep things in that you don't want to get wet, sandy or salty, such as your land clothes, phone, car keys and so on. Dry bags can also double usefully as containers for wet things in dry areas.

The Rest

Only buy scuba diving – specific equipment like a regulator, BCD and dive computer after you have "become a diver." rather than someone who has just tried diving. How will you know when you have made the transformation? Perhaps when you and others around you begin to describe you as a diver; when that becomes a term that at least partially defines you. Or when you find yourself planning weekends or entire vacations that focus on scuba diving to the exclusion of almost everything else. See the chapter "Scuba diving WILL change your life" for more examples. When you get to that point and before you start shopping, check out the Equipment section of my book Scuba Confidential. This will help you make all the right choices.

Start diving the right way by

being properly equipped.

§2

Learning to Dive

6. What to Expect from Your Beginner's Course

When you start learning to drive a car, you have a good idea of what you are going to do during the lessons. After all, you have probably been watching other people drive you around as a passenger all your life. Also, many people you know have had driving lessons and they can tell you in clear, easily understandable language what to expect.

But when you embark on a scuba diving course, you really do enter a whole new world. It is unlikely that you have spent any time at all watching divers do their thing. You may have friends who are already divers but, when you ask them about the course, the chances are that their explanations will be liberally littered with incomprehensible jargon such as regulator, narcosis and air depletion (sounds horrible) and bizarre acronyms like BCD, SPG and NDL.

Yes, it is true, after you have done a couple of training dives you will be chatting easily with other divers about concepts that would be completely indecipherable to the uninitiated. You will be talking about things like equalizing, mask clearing, neutral buoyancy, air sharing and back-rolling as if you have been one of the Scuba In-Crowd for years. But before you start diving, when you are still on the outside looking in, it is all a bit bewildering. This chapter aims to give you a good idea of just what you will be doing on your first diving course, without too many obscure references and alien concepts. If you do see a word you don't understand, the Jargon Buster at the end of Chapter 1 should help.

The Theory

Before you get into the water, you will need to learn a little diving theory so you know what happens to your body when you go underwater. You will also find out about scuba diving equipment, how it works and why we use it. There will be a little biology, a little physics and a little maths: nothing too mentally taxing but you might wish at times that you had listened more attentively in school.

The study material contains plenty of video of people diving, so you will be able to watch the process, the logistics and, importantly, the etiquette of a scuba dive. The video is not just background entertainment. It offers you a chance to see how to move underwater and notice important things such as how divers position themselves horizontally as they swim, how they keep their hands tucked in and how they manoeuvre with their legs, not their arms.

You can study diving theory either on the Internet, by watching a DVD, by reading a book, by listening to an instructor talk or via a combination of all these things. The general idea is that, if the information is presented to you in several ways, aurally, visually and practically, you will absorb it well, no matter what your personal learning preferences may be. Whichever media you use, the key person in the teaching process is always your instructor because he or she is the one who will answer any further questions you have after you have listened to and watched the theory presentations. And you will certainly have questions! So make sure the course you choose includes plenty of instructor contact time.

The Practice

Some instructors, dive centres and clubs present the theory in sections, interspersed with in-water sessions. Others give you the option of doing all the theory first before you get in the water.

Your first few dives will usually take place in a swimming pool or a protected spot in the sea or in a lake. Not all dive operations have access to a pool. Wherever you are, it should be a "pool-like" environment; that is the water should be shallow, calm, clear and sheltered from wind and waves. These are the sort of conditions that you should expect when you take your first few breaths underwater. You should not have to fight the elements.

The idea is that your initial forays underwater should be as comfortable and pleasurable as possible. You should be able to see the surface clearly at all times and your instructors and the other divers around you should always be in view. You should not have to deal with environmental complications such as moving water or poor visibility. This will leave you free to concentrate on enjoying the wonderful, almost-otherworldly experience of breathing underwater.

It may well be that later dives on the course will take place in darker, murkier, more testing conditions, but by then you will have a couple of hours on scuba behind you and have the skills and confidence to deal with these.

In a good course, every practical session will be run as a proper dive. You will be assigned another person to dive with, normally one of your course-mates. This person is your "buddy." You will get your equipment ready; check to make sure it is working properly and put it all on. You will then check that your buddy's equipment is working too and that they have not forgotten anything in the gearing up process. They, in turn, will also be checking that you have not forgotten anything. Reassuring isn't it?

You will enter the water, wait on the surface and then, after making sure your buddy is ready too, you will go underwater and just try swimming around. You will probably find that breathing is much easier than you thought it would be, but that keeping your balance and maintaining a fixed position in the water is much harder than you expected. If you have seen movies where trainee astronauts attempt to deal with weightlessness for the first time, you will have an idea of what awaits you. It will soon become much easier but, in the beginning, you will feel a little clumsy. Don't worry: it is the same for everyone.

You will learn how to use your equipment. Your instructor will also introduce you to problems that scuba divers commonly encounter and show you how to deal with them. Then you will have a chance to try out the techniques yourself.

It would be foolish to pretend that nothing can go wrong on a scuba dive. Equipment can fail and divers can make mistakes, so your instructor will be teaching you a) what can go wrong, b) what you should do if it does go wrong and c) how you can help your dive buddy if they have a problem during a dive. The procedures and techniques the instructor shows you are called "skills" and, in a good course, you will practise these a lot so that they become easy. Then, at the end of each dive, you will exit the water, remove your equipment, dismantle it, clean it and put it away. A full session should last a couple of hours.

The only way your first few water sessions may differ from a real life diving experience is that your instructor may ask you to go down and come back up again several times. In a normal scuba dive you make one descent at the beginning of the dive and one ascent at the end. You do not come up in the middle of a dive unless something goes wrong.

Making multiple descents and ascents in swimming pool sessions enables the instructor to brief you on what you will do on the dive in sections rather than all at once. It also gives you a lot of practice going down and coming back up, which is good, because these are the most important phases of every dive and it is essential that the procedures become natural and instinctive.

Do It Again and Again

Repetition is the key to becoming a good scuba diver. A course usually involves four or five pool or shallow water dives plus four or five dives in deeper, more exposed locations. This means you will be putting your equipment together and breaking it down 8 to 10 times during your course. Repeating everything several times should ensure you do not forget how to do it later, after you graduate, when there is no longer an instructor around.

In the later course dives, you will also be given plenty of opportunity to rehearse again the skills you learned in the pool so that they become second nature and so that you will react instinctively, correctly and without any drama if ever an emergency occurs. The biggest danger for any diver is panic, because, when someone panics, they do not think logically. In a diving situation, a person who panics will usually swim as fast as possible to the surface. This is the most common way that divers come to harm. Whenever you ascend from a dive, you must always be in control, relaxed, breathing normally and moving slowly.

The main aims of your initial course are to make sure that you become as comfortable as possible in the underwater environment and that you have enough knowledge and experience to be able to stay calm if a problem occurs.

Self Preservation

Among other things, you will learn to keep an eye on your equipment to make sure you always know how much air you have left. Yes, scuba divers breathe air underwater, not oxygen. This is something the newspapers always get wrong! You will learn what to do when your air supply is running low and you will learn how you can help your dive buddy if they forget to monitor their supply and run out of air completely. They in turn will be learning how to help you if you forget.

"What?" I can hear you saying. "How could anyone ever forget to check something as important as that?" Well, the ocean is full of distractions and you are only human. As many divers before you have discovered, it is all too possible to run out of air, so, as well as learning ways of ensuring that you always know how much air you have left, you have to know how to survive if the unthinkable happens.

You will also practise what to do if you get water in your mask, if your mask strap breaks, if the mouthpiece you breathe from breaks away or if something goes wrong with other bits of your equipment. All these are minor events but they may make you panic underwater if you are not aware of the possibility that they can happen and do not know how to respond if they do.

This is why the skills are covered in the course and why they are rehearsed multiple times. What might seem to be mountainous problems when you think of them now will be just minor inconveniences by the time you graduate as a diver.

Getting in the Swim

Your course will not just consist of problem-solving exercises, you will also be given plenty of time to swim around underwater in the equipment, getting used to the feeling of being submerged. You will be taught to adopt the long, slow breathing rhythm that keeps divers relaxed and comfortable and you will learn how to swim efficiently using only your legs and fins. You will also take your first steps along the path to the holy grail for scuba divers, the ability to stop all movement and remain motionless underwater, completely balanced, neither moving up nor down, as relaxed as if you were reclining in your favourite chair.

Although you do not use your arms and hands to actually swim when you are on scuba, you do use them for communication. So you will learn common hand signals that divers use to "talk" to each other underwater. This is important because, as I mentioned earlier, a dive normally takes place with one descent and one ascent. For a whole host of reasons that will become apparent on your course, divers cannot just pop to the surface for a chat from time to time mid – dive. So you use your hands. You may be surprised at how effective the hand signals are. You will also find out during the emergency drills you practise in your course, that, even when partially concealed behind a mask, your buddy's eyes can convey very important messages like "I have no air: please give me air!" extremely eloquently!

You should also learn how to use a safety sausage. This is a brightly coloured, inflatable device that you carry on every dive and use to show surface traffic where you are when you ascend. Many popular dive sites are very busy and boats come and go over the top of divers all the time. The boat drivers cannot see your bubbles and are usually moving fast. So, if you are not coming up a fixed anchor or mooring line, you need to raise a safety sausage first, before you surface, so that boats can avoid you. Your safety sausage also helps your dive boat see you when it comes to pick you up at the end of the dive.

Finally, you will have fun on your course! Dive instructors earn a living from teaching diving but they do not just do it for the money and you will find their infectious enthusiasm for this wonderful sport rubs off on you. You may be getting an education, but when your classroom is a swimming pool, a beach or a dive boat it certainly doesn't feel like school.

Start diving the right way by

knowing in advance what to expect from your course.

7. Choose Wisely

Strange as it may seem, most people do not choose the person who actually teaches them to dive. Instead, they just go into the dive shop or scuba club closest to their home and announce that they have decided they want to learn to dive. Or perhaps, on a whim, they make enquiries at the dive centre in the hotel where they are staying while they are on holiday. It is the club, shop or dive centre that then assigns them an instructor.

This may be what commonly happens but it is not necessarily what SHOULD happen. The decision as to which person will teach you to dive is far too important to be left to someone else or consigned to random chance. The dive centre, shop or club you approach and the scuba diver training agency they represent have some impact on the quality of the diving course you get. However, by far the most important factor is the person who actually teaches you. The personality, ability, dedication and professionalism of your dive instructor have a direct and crucial bearing on whether your scuba diving course is the first step on the path to a lifetime of adventure or whether you end up abandoning the sport early, having wasted a good deal of time and money.

Yes, it is THAT important!

Do not misunderstand me, no matter who your instructor is, you will almost certainly pass the course. Hardly anybody fails. But passing the course does not mean that you have been taught properly how to dive. Unfortunately, it can just mean that you were coached effectively enough to get through a multiple choice theory test and blindly imitate a few physical drills. The drop out rate in scuba diving following completion of initial training is enormous and much of this is down to poor preparation, (which I dealt with in Section One) or inadequate teaching. Sadly, some students do not even complete their course. They pull out halfway through when they discover too late that the instructor is not someone they can work with or is doing a bad job.

Dorene's Tale

Someone who did quit their course and who, tragically, never came back to give scuba diving another try was Dorene, a water baby of 60 who had always wanted to learn to scuba dive but had never found the time in her busy life. Now a successful businesswoman, she signed up for a course, and persuaded her husband to join her. Then they went shopping and bought a couple of thousand dollars worth of equipment from their local dive centre before the course began. The large financial commitment mirrored Dorene's determination finally to achieve her dream and become a diver.

In the pool both she and her husband managed all the skills with aplomb. They even achieved mastery of a confidence-testing skill sequence requiring them to remove their equipment at the deep end then surface, take a breath and descend to put it all back on again. However, during the final pool session the instructor asked the students to put their equipment on while standing at the side of the pool, but in a different way than they were used to. They were to put their arms through the straps of their BCD then swing the equipment up and over their head, slipping it on as they did so.

Dorene tried this a couple of times, but only succeeded in banging her head with the cylinder each time and nearly dropping everything. As she stood there bruised and battered, the instructor approached and announced none too gently that if she wanted to become a real diver, she was going to have to learn how to do this. It is worth pointing out here that this particular task is not actually required by any scuba diver training agency. It was completely a personal foible of this particular instructor.

That evening, thinking about the terrible day she had had, Dorene realised she just did not have the physical strength to lift that amount of weight easily over her head and decided that evidently scuba diving was not for her. Distressed and disappointed, she abandoned the course, as did her husband, and six months later they sold all their almost unused equipment at a substantial loss.

Dorene is not alone. Over the years, a number of people, many of whom are excellent swimmers with an interest in the natural world, have told me that they tried scuba diving once but found that it was not for them. On being questioned more closely they say that they felt uncomfortable, inadequate or clumsy; that it did not come naturally to them or they did not think they would make good divers.

They blame themselves but it is not them who are to blame. The fact is that the person who was tasked with teaching them to dive managed to do such a poor job that they were put off ever doing it again. They either chose the wrong instructor or were not given the opportunity to choose. Not all dive instructors teach the same way. Not all teaching styles will suit you. Your dive instructor needs to be someone you trust, someone you have faith in, someone you actually like. Think back to your school days. We all learned better when we had a teacher with whom we felt some empathy.

Making it too Hard

Anecdotal examples abound of how, for some unfathomable reason, many dive instructors seem to put a lot of effort into making learning to dive as difficult as possible.

A lady named Sarah once told me that for her first pool session with a very large and successful dive centre in the Caribbean, she was not offered a wetsuit for her pool sessions and ended the day with knee and elbow scrapes. She also had raw patches on her shoulders where the BCD harness had chafed her skin. The BCD fitted her so badly and she was so heavily weighted that, on the surface, even when her BCD was fully inflated, her chin would still be at water level while the shoulder straps hovered above her ears.

The depth gauge on Sarah's console did not work and when she pointed this out, her instructor just said, "it doesn't matter, we are in a pool; we know how deep it is!" She cancelled the course after the first day but fortunately she did not give up. She found another dive centre and another instructor and is now a proud and certified new diver.

How to Choose

Obviously a good first step in choosing an instructor is to ask for recommendations from people who have already done the course and whose opinion you trust.

Note, however, that this is just a first step. Your friends are not necessarily a reliable source. There is a good chance that their own diving instructor is the only one they have ever met so they have no point of comparison and are unable to be objective. They are also not you. Your learning preferences may be very different from theirs.

Once you have a recommendation or two, the next thing to do is talk to the instructors directly, either by phone or in person. Interview them. Although they may not think of it in this way, they are technically applying for the job of teaching you to dive. Ask all the questions you can think of and assess their response. Do their answers reassure you or do they fill you with further doubts? Does it sound like they care? After all, if they don't have time for you BEFORE you have paid for your course, then you cannot expect to receive the attention you need AFTER they have pocketed your money!

Try and get a chance to observe at first hand each instructor's attitude to training and personal dive skills. Ask the instructors if you can attend a swimming pool session as an observer or pay to go out snorkelling on a boat trip when they are teaching or guiding. Watch them at work. Do they devote 100% of their attention to the divers in their charge? Do you find their personality and approach to work sympathetic? Above all, are they professional?

Professional?

As a non-diver, it may be difficult for you to judge whether dive instructors are being professional or not. Let me try to help. Here are some things that will strongly suggest that you are in the presence of someone who really knows what they are doing when they are teaching beginners.

1. The student divers are wearing equipment and thermal protection that look similar to the equipment that the instructor is using.

2. The student divers are working in pairs when they put their equipment on and take it off, helping each other and double-checking each other.

3. The student divers put their gear together themselves before EVERY water session and break it down again after EVERY water session. (*The only exception to this would be if the students were not actually learning to become qualified divers but were just undergoing a dive experience to see if they liked it. In this case the instructor and staff would take care of equipment assembly and disassembly.*)

4. The instructor lets the students work together independently, only intervening when a mistake goes uncorrected.

5. The instructor is present ALL the time when the students are in or close to the water.

6. The instructor works tirelessly teaching the divers their self-rescue skills, encouraging them to repeat them frequently so that they remember them.

7. The instructor talks to the students in clear language, rather than incomprehensible "scuba-speak."

8. The students look like they understand what the instructor is saying. There is genuine communication between them.

9. The instructor is willing to spend extra time personally with a student who is having difficulty with something.

10. Underwater, the student divers are swimming almost horizontally, rather than at a 45-degree angle with head up and feet down.

11. The divers' hoses are secured to their BCD and are not hanging down beneath them and dragging on the bottom of the pool or seabed.

12. The students spend a large part of their time swimming or floating motionless in mid-water. They do not spend most of their dive kneeling on the bottom.

13. The instructor makes sure the students keep their arms tucked in front of them or by their sides when they swim.

14. The instructor devotes time to making sure the students know how to fin with purpose and in at least two different ways.

Finally, 15. The instructor is positive at all times. They do not criticise; they do not blame; they do not ignore student questions; they are always ready to explain. They keep moving but do not rush. They do not waste time; they are organised and, if they are teaching more than two students at the same time, they are smart enough to have an assistant on hand to help them.

Value

Scuba diving courses do not cost the same all over the world. To add to the confusion, even when you ask around on the same beach or in the same town, you may be quoted prices that vary widely. How can you ever know if you are getting a good deal?

In the world of scuba diving, rest assured that you get what you pay for. So, once you have found an instructor who is professional and caring and seems to be someone you would work well with, pay what they ask. If they seem to be more expensive than others you have found, this is probably because they like to teach classes with fewer students so they can offer more personal attention, are good at what they do and pay their assistants well.

The fact that an instructor can charge more and still stay in business, may also mean that your research efforts have been successful and your good feelings about the instructor are well founded. So, if the course is more expensive than you originally budgeted for then save up your money and do it when you can afford it, rather than seek out a cheaper alternative.

When you are on holiday, never choose a dive course just because it sounds like a bargain. A cheap course will ALWAYS mean rushed lectures, short dive times, a tight schedule and little time for questions, individual assessment or remedial work. If the course seems cheaper than courses offered elsewhere, it is certain that the instructor will cut corners. You may not even notice when this happens or know which corners have been cut, but if someone in a resort environment is selling a course that is cheaper than their competitors, then it is certain they will be short-changing the students somewhere along the line.

Always ask if learning materials, equipment, boat dives and any extra tuition necessary are included in the quoted price. They should be.

Having said all this, be aware that, if you are learning to dive at home, a cheap price may not necessarily be a sign of a poor quality course. It may simply reflect the fact that the instructor only works in diving part-time or is a dive club volunteer.

Currency

This is a key factor that is often overlooked. All scuba instructors can teach people to dive, but not all instructors are used to working with new divers. You should choose someone who has significant recent experience teaching people to dive from scratch.

You want to learn from people who know what they are talking about but the length of time that an instructor has been teaching may not always be a reliable indicator. As in many professional fields, after a while dive instructors tend to specialise. Also, someone who has been doing the same thing for a long time can become jaded and set in their ways. Or they might just be too successful and in-demand to devote their whole attention to you. Newer instructors are often more enthusiastic, attentive to detail, open to new methods and ready to put in the extra time.

Which Training Agency?

There is a good chance that, unless you have access to scuba diving magazines or do online research in diver forums, you may think that the only scuba training agency is PADI, whose slogan is "The Way the World Learns to Dive." Some people even refer to becoming a qualified scuba diver as "getting your PADI."

PADI is the only industry organisation that advertises to the non-diving world but, in fact, there are hundreds of scuba training agencies. The other ones confine their marketing activities to people who are already divers. Some operate in only a limited number of languages or only in one or two countries.

What you learn in your course does not differ much between agencies. Usually, an instructor will represent one agency only but, even if they represent two or three agencies, the important elements of the classes they teach will be identical.

An element that really differs between training agencies is the speed and level of commitment with which they have applied themselves to the Internet revolution. Some have embraced it wholeheartedly. Some have almost ignored it. Some pretend to offer online education but do not really understand what is required.

If you are used to studying online, benefitting from access to a limitless range of high-quality content in various media forms and liaising and sharing constantly with teachers, mentors and fellow students while you learn, then the way scuba diving theory is taught may feel somewhat "old-world." Whiteboards, (even blackboards,) fat, heavy printed books and DVDs are still the norm.

You may be comfortable with this, but if following a more up-to-date way of learning is important to you, you will want to know in advance what options each agency gives you. So include questions on this in your instructor interview.

Club or Dive Centre? Home or Away?

Much is made about whether it is better to learn to dive while you are on holiday or whether it is better to schedule your course at home over evenings and weekends around a normal working life. In terms of the quality of the course, there is really little difference. You are just as likely to find a great instructor that suits you in a local dive shop in Madison, Wisconsin as you are on a beach in Koh Tao, Thailand or a dive club in Oxford, England.

It depends rather on you, your lifestyle, your readiness and how you prefer to learn. Doing a scuba diving course at home gives you more time for reflection between theory and diving sessions and allows you to be much more flexible and learn at your own pace. The disadvantage is often that distractions from other areas of your life can intrude and prevent you concentrating on the course or giving it the attention you should.

If you learn to dive while you are on holiday, you have limited time and less flexibility in terms of the course schedule. Depending on where you choose to go, the ocean may be warmer than at home, but temperature is not really a key factor. Wherever you learn to dive, you will be given enough thermal protection to keep you warm for the duration of your dives.

Be aware too that the water in sunny, tropical destinations is not always as warm as you might expect. For example, in Egypt, a common warm water destination for European divers, few swimming pools are heated and, in winter, new divers can experience their first few breaths underwater in temperatures as low as 14C (57F.)

If it suits you, you can learn by combining both options, home and away. Many local dive clubs and dive centres can offer schedules whereby you learn the theory and do your swimming pool dives locally, then join a trip to a tropical destination for your training dives in the ocean.

Start diving the right way by

choosing wisely.

8. Embrace the Technology

Recently I met up with a couple who had just completed their second scuba diving course. They wanted advice about buying a dive computer and I asked which brand they had used during their training to date. They said they had not actually used a computer yet. During their beginner's course, they had planned all the dives using decompression tables and in their advanced class they had been told that they did not need a computer because their instructor had one. After each dive, the instructor would read out the dive data and they would copy it dutifully into their logbooks.

Theirs is not an isolated case. As far as technology is concerned, many dive operators are still living in the last century; and not the final decade of the last century either. Dive computers have been universally available to scuba divers for over 25 years now. Today a dive computer is not an optional extra: it is as standard a part of a diver's equipment as a regulator or mask.

The primary purpose of scuba training, right from the start, is to teach divers to be self-reliant, to be in charge of their own dives, to be independent parts of a team of two (or more) divers, each one able to manage their own dives and help any one of the others if they get into difficulty.

Your dive computer is the key to achieving those goals. If you do not have one then you are dependent on someone else. However, you are the one who should be in control, no matter what level of experience you have.

When you learn to dive, you should be given a dive computer to use right from the beginning, even in confined water sessions. Your instructor should give you a full set of equipment for every dive so you have as much opportunity as possible to get used to it. You should be taught how dive computers work and how to use them conservatively. You should also learn how to use decompression tables and refer to both tables AND your computer when planning and reviewing your course dives. A good instructor will use the comparison as a platform for a whole host of valuable teaching points.

"If students want to use a dive computer, they should buy one," some operators might protest. This is unfair. It is as unrealistic to require a new diver to buy their own computer, as it is to expect them to buy their own regulator. They need first to decide that scuba diving is a sport that they will stick with before they start investing serious sums of money in it.

Besides, scuba diving is a service industry so, if customers want a service, such as the option of renting a dive computer, and they are willing to pay for it, then they should be able to do this.

There's No Rational Excuse

So why do so many operations not offer rental computers. Does it all come down to a certain reluctance to move with the times, a systemic resistance to change? Are they afraid that divers who rent computers will lose them or steal them? If so, why not take a credit card deposit or include the computers in consoles along with the submersible pressure gauge and compass?

The excuse, "you don't need one because your dive guide, divemaster or instructor has one" goes against all the tenets of safe diving. Dive professionals who use that line are violating accepted core safety standards and are either ignorant or dishonest. You will never see experienced divers or professionals consciously enter the water without their own computer.

What to Do?

So, what should you do if your dive operator does not stock computers for rent and you are not yet ready to buy one? Give your business to a dive operator who does offer the service and will take the time to show you how to use the computer before you take it out.

Then, when you have decided that scuba diving is definitely for you, buy your own.

Start diving the right way by

embracing the technology.

9. Twelve Ways You Can Help Your Instructor

When you sign up for classes with any academic institution these days, you are likely to be given a student contract to sign. By signing the contract, you agree to a certain code of behaviour that will make sure you get the most from the classes and help your teachers to help you, so to speak.

When you start your scuba diving course, it is unlikely that you will be given a contract although it would be a good idea for instructors and dive centres to adopt the practice. Many of the provisions of a typical academic student contract apply equally to diver training; plus a few others that are more subject specific.

The list in this chapter will have instructors nodding their heads enthusiastically. If you want to get on the right side of the person teaching you to dive, there is no need to bring an apple to class. Just make sure you do these things.

1. If you are learning with a friend, spouse or partner, don't bring your relationship to class. This applies especially when you are underwater. Don't interfere; leave the teaching to the teacher. If one of you thinks the other is doing something wrong, leave it for the instructor to spot and fix. If the instructor does not act, it doesn't mean they haven't seen whatever it is you think you have spotted. It means either that you are wrong and your significant other is doing just fine or that the instructor is giving them time to work it out for themselves.

Besides, at this early stage in your diving career, you have enough on your own plate without worrying about what other people are doing. If anyone needs your help, they will ask for it. Otherwise, concentrate on your own diving. The last thing any instructor needs is a couple arguing underwater, bubbling at each other incomprehensibly through their regulators. If you find you become anxious underwater about something another diver is doing, the chances are that, rather than feeling genuine concern for them, you are actually just transferring anxiety about your own situation.

2. Follow the advice in Section One of this book regarding pre-course preparation, so you are ready for your course.

3. Be organised before and during class. Being meticulous about your equipment and establishing pre-dive and post-dive routines are excellent safety strategies and it is best to start as you mean to go on. If, like most of us, your world is normally chaotic, let your scuba diving time be an oasis of calm and order in the storm.

4. Remove other responsibilities from your schedule during course hours so that you can focus only on scuba diving. Don't take calls; don't check messages. If you have important people

in your life such as children, staff or colleagues, who depend on you being constantly accessible, then find someone to assume that role for you while you are learning to dive. Later, when you have become a diver, you are going to have to find people to do this for you anyway, as you are not going to be accessible while you are out on a boat or underwater. This may actually be one of the reasons you are learning to scuba dive: to get away and enjoy a little me time!

5. Be prepared to allocate several hours between course sessions to review what you have done in the previous session, do some private study and prepare for the next session. Get plenty of sleep. You will find that there is a lot to learn, in terms of both knowledge and physical skills, so you will need to be well rested to be able to assimilate it all as well as you can.

6. Don't embark on the course thinking that there will be things that you cannot do. If you have ticked all the boxes in section one of this book regarding health, watermanship and snorkelling practice, you can accomplish everything that you will be asked to do in your scuba diving course. Millions of people just like you have passed this way and have become very successful scuba divers. There is no reason why you can't follow their example.

Remove all negativity from your mind. This includes any negativity you may have received from well-meaning non-diving "friends," who cannot resist passing on their groundless or imaginary fears when they hear you are going to scuba dive. Concentrate and don't let your mind wander. Watch what your instructor does, listen to what they tell you, focus on what you are doing and prepare to be amazed at how well you do and how natural it quickly becomes to go underwater and STAY THERE!

7. Your instructor will be working hard to avoid and remove all obstacles to learning. Do not become an obstacle yourself. It is very hard for an instructor to help you overcome a problem if you have just invented it yourself and it does not exist anywhere except inside your head.

8. When, despite all that focussing, listening and concentration, you make a mistake, (as you will because you are only human), don't worry about it. You will not come up with a new way of doing something wrong that your instructors have not seen before. They have seen everything. So brush it off, listen to the explanation of what you did wrong, watch the instructor's re-demonstration and try again. You will get it. Occasionally, you may get a mental block about something but, very often, after you have gone away and reviewed everything in your mind, the blockage clears and you come back the next day and get it right first time.

9. Being early for a session not only means you don't miss anything, it means you are in as relaxed a frame of mind as possible. Arriving with all your reading up to date and any "homework" completed means you will be able to participate actively in the course. It also means that any questions you ask will be meaningful and relevant. You will not be wasting the instructor's and your fellow students' time with questions you would know the answers to already if you had completed your assignments.

10. Obey the etiquette of scuba diving, especially the sections concerning interaction with your fellow divers and with the marine environment.

11. Don't come to class with your head filled with diving tips and tricks that an "experienced" neighbour or office colleague has given you. Whisper it quietly but they may not be as

experienced as they make themselves out to be. "In the land of the blind, the one-eyed man is king," or so the saying goes.

12. Don't Hold Your Breath

The twelfth and final way you can help your instructor requires a more involved explanation.

Earlier in the book I talked about my friend who would take a deep breath before she turned her face into the shower. Most of us tend to do the same in such circumstances or when we duck our head beneath the water in a bath tub.

You do not hold your breath when you go under water on a scuba dive. There is no need. After all, you are taking a substantial air supply down with you. When you are on the surface, on scuba and ready to descend, adopt a long, slow, calm, relaxed breathing pattern. Don't even try to descend until you have got this breathing pattern going.

There is a sequence to follow when you want to descend on a scuba dive. You will be taught this sequence and practise it many times in your course. The one element in the sequence that is sometimes not given enough emphasis is the need to start a long, slow exhalation as you descend and continue exhaling until you are couple of metres / a few feet underwater. Then you breathe in.

The reason you exhale as you descend is to become negatively buoyant and you need to be negatively buoyant to get yourself underwater. The several litres of air you keep in your lungs when you hold your breath are enough to stop you going down, even if you get everything else about the descent sequence right.

The same applies if you are taking quick, shallow breaths in and out. When you breathe like that, you never empty your lungs sufficiently to be able to descend.

"Ah," you may say, "but once I am underwater and take a breath, I will just pop up again."

"Ah," I will reply, "that's where you're wrong! Even when you are only a couple of metres / a few feet below the surface, the surrounding water pressure will compress your wetsuit and help further empty your BCD, as long as you continue to press the deflate button. So you are no longer as positively buoyant as you were on the surface. That means you can inhale without popping up again.

In your class, a good instructor will of course tell you all this but I mention it here so that you are aware in advance of the importance of exhaling as you make your initial descent. Remembering this one thing will make your initial dives go so much more smoothly and help your instructor enormously.

When confronted with trainee divers who try to descend while holding a full breath, or who breathe so quickly that they never really empty their lungs, busy instructors will often solve the problem by adding more weight to the students' weightbelt, simply to get them under water so that they can make progress with the class.

If you dive with more weight than you need, you use up more energy than necessary so you get tired more quickly. You also use up more air than you normally would so your dives are shorter. Furthermore, you will find it impossible to maintain a horizontal position in the water as the extra weight around your waist makes your legs hang down below you. This in turn makes it harder to swim properly.

By remembering to breathe out as you descend, you will make it unnecessary for your instructor to give you more weight than you need and you will start diving the right way by wearing exactly the right amount.

Start diving the right way by

helping your instructor help you.

10. The Six Essentials

Your first scuba diving course takes you on a momentous journey from permanent landlubber to temporary denizen of the watery depths. You have a lot to learn in terms of knowledge and physical skills as you make this life-changing transition. Indeed, there is so much that it may all seem overwhelming at first. It can sometimes be hard to distinguish the really important things from those that are just nice to know.

To be a safe, successful scuba diver, the following six elements are the things you have to concentrate on mastering more than anything else. As you will see, they are all inter-connected. Improvement in one area will lead to similar progress in all the others.

Focus on these things, get them right and everything else will fall into place.

1. Breathing

Despite what many new divers are told when they begin, you do not breathe "normally" when you are underwater on scuba. The manuals only say that to try to reassure new students that diving is easy and to dispel any fears they may have about not being able to breathe.

When you are underwater you are breathing air under pressure, so the air is denser than the air you breathe from the atmosphere when you are on land. You are also breathing through your regulator, which is an artificial device that extends the distance between your lungs and the source of the air. This gap is called "dead air space."

Because of these two factors, if you breathe as you do on land, that is, haphazardly and without thinking about it, turbulence within the dead air space will prevent much of the air you inhale from reaching your lungs. You will just breathe it all out again, without the important oxygen-carbon dioxide exchange having taken place. This is not a good thing because this exchange is the whole point of breathing.

So, to breathe efficiently underwater, you have to develop a controlled long, slow breathing style, pull the dense air down deep into your lungs with each inhalation and then expel it in a long, slow exhalation.

Breathe from your diaphragm, rather than your chest. How do you do this? When you inhale, push your stomach all the way out so that it distends to allow your lungs to expand and draw in as much air as possible. Then, when you exhale, compress your stomach muscles to reduce your lung volume to a minimum. Breathe out slowly and continuously until it feels like there is no air left to exhale. Then breathe in again. You don't need to pause between breaths; just let your breathing be a constant cycle of long ins followed by long outs.

Breathing from the diaphragm does take a little getting used to but you do not have to be actually diving to practise the technique. This is something you can do any time, anywhere, while you are riding in a train, sitting in your car in a traffic jam or watching TV. At home, a good exercise is to lie on the floor, put a book on your stomach and focus on moving the book up and down by slowly breathing in and out. As you do this, breathe with your lips pursed, as they would be around your regulator mouthpiece. Draw the air in slowly and release it slowly.

2. Relaxing

The extended cycle of deep inhalation and full exhalation will also ensure that the gas exchange I mentioned earlier is as effective as possible. When you breathe like this, more of the oxygen you breathe in will be transferred from your lungs to your bloodstream and more carbon dioxide will be removed from your body.

This benefits you in two major ways. First, your body needs oxygen. Second, a build up of carbon dioxide makes you stressed and anxious. When you exhale efficiently, you reduce your body's carbon dioxide levels and this makes you more relaxed and less prone to anxiety.

Being relaxed when you dive enables you to be more attentive, puts you in a good frame of mind to deal calmly with any emergency that may take place and reduces considerably your tendency to panic. The greatest threat to any new diver comes from an uncontrolled ascent. Every diver knows this from the start, yet uncontrolled ascents are still much too common.

Why? Because panic over-rides the intellect and induces people to do things they would never do if their brain were in charge. Reduce as much as possible the likelihood that you will panic by acquiring a long, slow breathing habit and learning to relax underwater by adopting techniques like visualisation.

Visualisation is an important tool. Before a scuba dive, sit in a quiet place and think about the dive ahead. Think positive thoughts; imagine all the wonderful things you are going to experience and picture a successful dive in your mind. See yourself as you descend, in control, checking all your gear is in place, keeping a long, slow breathing rhythm, maintaining good buoyancy control, looking around at the environment and staying in touch with your dive team. Then focus your thoughts on the dive itself. Visualise yourself feeling comfortable, being aware and checking the status of your computer and submersible pressure gauge from time to time. See yourself making a slow, safe and controlled ascent with a safety stop, finally establishing positive buoyancy on the surface and ending the dive with plenty of air.

Visualisation is also an effective weapon to deploy against apprehension. It is not uncommon for new divers to be apprehensive about their ability to cope with a situation and it can be dangerous to begin a dive in this state of mind, as it does not take much for the apprehension to turn into panic. Your scuba diving course teaches you how to deal with anything that might go wrong while you are underwater. By reflecting during your visualisation about what could happen and realising that you know exactly how to deal with it, you eliminate apprehension, grow in self-confidence and can approach the dive with a positive, relaxed attitude.

3. Controlling Buoyancy

I referred to the concept of good buoyancy control in the previous section. This is diver-speak for being in complete charge of where you are and where you go when you are underwater. Something that floats is referred to as positively buoyant; something that sinks is negatively buoyant. The nirvana sought by scuba divers is neutral buoyancy, the state of being suspended in water, neither floating nor sinking.

When you first start diving, you may feel extraordinarily clumsy. This is how most people are when they first go underwater. At one point, even the professionals, who hang effortlessly in mid-water in total control while you flail and roll around, were once just as awkward and ungainly as you are now.

In your class, you will be taught a variety of techniques to help you acquire good buoyancy control skills. Practise these at every opportunity. Unless you are learning with an instructor one-on-one, you will always have down time while the instructor is working with one of your classmates. Use this time to watch how the professionals control their movement and position in the water while they are working. Notice how their ability to remain completely stable or "fly" underwater comes down to fin management, body management and breath management. These are the holy trinity of buoyancy control. See the professionals' mastery of the environment not as something magical and unattainable, but as something you too can and should acquire. Ask your instructors if they mind if, while they are working with other divers in your group, you work on the skills you have already been taught. Just like most things in life, the more you do it, the better you will get at it.

4. Watching

In the same way as you watch your instructors intently while you are learning, be similarly attentive to your environment when you dive and remain alert to everything that is going on around you. Yes, monitor your gauges as you were taught but don't become fixated on them. Just as you do when you walk around on land, look where you are going and, if you are planning to return by the same route, turn round occasionally to see what it will look like on the way back.

As you are descending, look down to see what sort of topography awaits you. Are you going down towards sand, reef, rock or seaweed? Are there other divers below you? When you plan to ascend, look up before you go up and be more cautious the closer you get to the surface, where sharp and potentially deadly threats await in the form of boat hulls, boat propellers, jet skis and other marine traffic.

In your daily life, you have developed sensitive, invisible antennae that you deploy subconsciously as you go about your business. They enable you, for example, to cross roads safely, avoid potholes in the pavement, dodge kids on skateboards or spot people who need your help or may need your seat on a busy train more than you do. Don't retract these antennae when you go underwater. In fact, if possible, extend them even further.

New divers often seem to be focussed on a movie streaming inside their minds rather than on what is going on around them. They are in a new environment and the novelty makes them less attentive. This is similar to the lack of attention typically exhibited by tourists that makes them such good targets for thieves and fraudsters. There are no pickpockets underwater but if you are dreaming, lost in wonder and not watching what is happening around you, you are not in control of your dive.

I warned earlier about being fixated on your gauges. Your computer and submersible pressure gauge can be compared to your mobile phone. They are vital for conveying important information but a distraction if you refer to them constantly. Just like someone walking down a city street with their eyes on the screen in their hands, you can easily miss what is happening around you or suddenly look up from your device and find yourself where you do not want to be. When you are a new diver, you may find it incredible that a diver could find himself or herself separated from their group, when it is so important to stay with them. "How could that possibly happen?" you may ask. Allowing your attention to wander or getting caught up in absent-minded thoughts; that's how.

Watch what the other people you are diving with are doing in the water and you will become a better buddy. You may even perceive problems they are having before they do themselves and this will enable you to put yourself in a position to lend assistance if necessary. Here's an example.

The other day, I was following a diver around a huge submerged rock. She was not part of my group and seemed to be perfectly relaxed and comfortable. Suddenly I noticed that her position in the water had changed. Her fins had dropped towards the seabed and she was waggling them pointlessly, not going anywhere. I quickly swam closer and saw that a sea whip coral had got entangled with her regulator hose and pulled the regulator from her mouth. I watched as she reached down calmly for her back up regulator, put in her mouth and then turned to see what had happened. Once she saw the problem, she set about disentangling herself.

She freed her main regulator from the grip of the coral, put it back in her mouth, stowed her back up regulator away again and set off to catch up with the rest of her group, who were now out of sight. She was safe, she had solved the problem herself and she had not even noticed me just behind her. But, because I had been alert, I had been ready to offer help if she needed it. This is what being a good buddy is all about. Underwater, every diver is potentially a buddy that may need help: even if they do not even know you are there.

5. Finning

Your fins are propulsion devices, buoyancy controllers and stabilisers. When required, they can be finely tipped quill pens or delicate precision instruments. At other times they can be broad paintbrushes and power tools. You use your fins like you use the pedals when you are driving a car, except that, not only do fins enable you to speed up, slow down, stop and change gear, they help you steer as well. Your fins do it all. For scuba diving purposes, your hands and arms are simply for signalling and are tucked away when you have nothing to "say."

This is not simply a question of bizarre protocol, nor is it just that if you allow your hands to wander you may strike another diver or disturb the fragile eco-system you are swimming through. You tuck your arms away primarily so that you are more streamlined in the water. This reduces the amount of energy you need to use to swim and thus reduces the amount of air you use. Conserving air means your supply lasts longer. Also, scuba diving is not the same as tightrope walking. Waving your hands and arms around under water will actually make you more unstable rather than less. As I said earlier, a diver's stability comes primarily from buoyancy control.

Learning how to fin properly requires a great deal of concentration and effort. Most people find they have to move their leg muscles in ways they have never moved before. Unfortunately, not a great deal of time is spent on finning in early diver training. Often, there simply isn't enough time. This is why I recommend that new divers work on finning before they start their scuba class and I give some examples of different finning techniques you can try in the chapter "Snorkelling Dos and Don'ts."

Every fin stroke must be made consciously and have a purpose. All too often, even experienced divers allow their fins to reflect their state of mind. In the story I told in "Watching" earlier, the thing that alerted me to the fact that the diver had a problem was the abrupt change in her finning style. A tell-tale sign of an anxious diver is leg and fin movement with no purpose. It is as if their legs are reflecting the chaos of their confused mind.

So, as well as learning how to fin; learn how NOT to fin as well. In your scuba class, you will be told that if you ever feel like you are about to panic underwater, the first thing you do is stop all movement. Most of all, this means, "stop moving your fins." Get into the habit of staying motionless in the water. Only use your fins when you actually want to go somewhere.

6. Looking Closely

To get the most out of scuba diving, learn to look beyond the reef and notice how the fish and animals behave. On shipwrecks, learn to identify parts of the vessel and spot the artefacts that remain undisturbed amid the silt-covered metal. To borrow a common phrase, learn to see the wood for the trees. This means you have to get closer, which is where all of the other six essentials come in very handy. A key goal to aim for is to develop these skills to the point where you are able to remain absolutely still in the water without consciously thinking about how you are doing it. Then you can concentrate your attention completely on what you are looking at. Most divers do not actually start looking in detail at the things they are swimming past until comparatively late in their diving lives. However, there is no reason at all why new divers should not, right from the start, work on developing the skills to enable them to do this.

Start diving the right way by

focussing on the six essentials.

§3

Now You Can Dive

11. Taking Responsibility

Scuba diving is a team sport. When you first start diving you are taught about the buddy system and told that you should never dive alone. This is good advice. There are definite benefits to diving with another person or in a team. Human beings are social animals, after all. We like to share our experiences and we derive emotional security from the company of others.

The Buddy System

The buddy system is a concept that is much misunderstood so I should take a little time here to clarify things. In my book for more advanced divers, *Scuba Confidential,* I amplify these thoughts in an entire chapter dedicated to the topic.

When you first learned about the buddy system, like many people, you probably found it reassuring that, when you dive, someone, your buddy, will be there by your side to help you if something goes wrong. You may not have considered that there is a complementary aspect. For the buddy system to function as it should, each diver, and this includes you too, has to be so skilled and capable that they can run their own dive on auto-pilot, while simultaneously giving their full attention to helping a buddy in difficulty. Not only must a diver accept complete responsibility for their own dive, therefore, they also have to be prepared to take some responsibility for their buddy's dive too.

Make this your primary learning goal during your first 20 dives or so. You should aim to reach a level where you can take care of yourself with such competence that you can come to the aid of another diver in an emergency if required, without compromising your safety (or making the other diver's situation even worse than it was before you arrived!)

You do not dive with other people so that they can take care of you in the event that something goes wrong. That is YOUR job. This is why you are taught self-rescue skills in your initial training. In your first scuba class you are told how to avoid and anticipate problems with the diving environment and your equipment. You are also taught how to manage these problems if they occur and how to make sure they do not lead to you coming to harm. This is the most important aspect of the course; everything else is secondary. After that, it is just a matter of practice, both in further classes and outside class, to get yourself into a position where you are completely responsible for your own diving and not dependent on others to keep you safe.

You will not reach this level immediately. Nobody can. During your first 20 dives, you can be forgiven for still finding your way and needing a more experienced buddy, a guide or an instructor to keep a watchful eye on you. In the chapter "What's Next?" I suggest what those first 20 dives should look like and recommend that, at the end of this period, you should sign up for a Rescue Diver course. This is the course that turns you into a thinking, independent diver, with your thoughts no longer focussed only on your own safety and survival, but also on the safety of those you are diving with. Many divers find that this is the point at which they realise what it takes to be a "good buddy."

Instructors and Guides

"But," I hear you cry, "It was not my idea to become an independent diver. I was planning to do all my diving with a guide or an instructor around." The main problem with this plan is that, once you are a qualified diver and have 20 dives or so in your log, the general assumption among professional divers will be that you know how to look after yourself.

In any event, you should never put complete responsibility for your safety on a dive in the hands of someone else, no matter who they are. The only exception to this is when you sign up for a diving course that takes you into an environment or to depths where you have no prior experience, and where you cannot reasonably be expected to be self-reliant. In such circumstances, you pay an instructor to take the responsibility for your safety. You also pay the instructor to give you the tools to survive in a similar environment after the course is finished, when the instructor is no longer there.

When you are on a guided dive, it is not always the dive guide's primary job to look after you. Indeed, sometimes it may not be their job at all. Some dive operations provide guides only to show you where to go or to find interesting marine life for you to see and photograph. Your safety is entirely your responsibility. Even if the guide is charged with a safety support role, they will usually have other divers under their care as well. So, they may not be there when you need them. They may be busy helping someone else. But if you have the knowledge, skills and experience to be a confident, independent diver, then, whatever happens, you can look after yourself. As cave diving explorer and deep diving pioneer Tom Mount famously said, "only you can swim for you. Only you can think for you."

Mandy's Tale

Even very experienced buddies make mistakes and the following story illustrates this very well. A few years ago, Mandy was a new diver and had never done a night dive before. It was summertime and waters in the south of England were calm that evening and as warm as they ever get. She takes up the story.

 "It was a regular club dive and I was partnered with our diving officer, probably the most experienced diver in the club. The plan was to make a shore dive from the fisherman's slip on the south side of Swanage Bay and head towards the main pier. My buddy told me he wanted to catch a couple of flat-fish to take home for supper."

 "It was a dark, moonless night and, as we entered the water, I was feeling excited, albeit a little nervous. I could see the lights of Swanage town off to our left and, ahead of us, the glow in the water from the torches of a couple of other divers. After the usual equipment checks, the diving officer handed me my end of our buddy line and I clipped it on to my BCD. We had the line to make sure that if our torches failed or we ran into very bad visibility, we would not get separated. We swam out on the surface a little then descended to a depth of around 6m (20ft.) I remember being surprised at how much I could see, despite the fact that it was night-time. My buddy was on something of a mission to catch his flat-fish, so I decided my job was just to fin along next to him and see if I could help him find some."

"About 15 minutes into the dive, he signalled that we should go up. On reaching the surface, he explained he just wanted to check where we were. After he got his bearings, we descended again and swam in a different direction. Five minutes later, we went back up again, then back down once more. On the bottom, we continued in the same direction, this time finning much harder."

"Eventually, we ascended for the third and last time and my buddy suggested we fin on our backs on the surface towards the shore. Sensing an edge of concern in his voice, I looked around and saw that the lights of Swanage seemed to be moving away from us! I finned as hard as I could for what seemed like an age and, finally, we reached the shore at Peveril Ledge, a long way from both where we had started and where we had intended to go. Completely exhausted, we crawled out of the water on our hands and knees. Once we got our breath back, we headed out on foot for the pier to find our club mates, who were very relieved to see us, having finished their dives long before."

"In Swanage, as the tide comes in, it hits the north end of the bay, then sweeps back round towards the pier and out to sea. If we had followed our original dive plan and just headed for the pier we would have been alright, but my buddy had taken us off course in his quest for flat-fish and we had been picked up by a strong offshore current which had swept us off towards Peveril race and the open sea."

"I was pretty calm throughout the whole event but this was only because I had no idea how much danger we were really in.

It was only much later that I understood how bad it could have been. I was a novice and had put my life in the hands of another diver without a second thought. This taught me that I needed to be self-sufficient and not to put blind faith in others, no matter how experienced they are."

As Mandy found out, no matter who your buddy is, you still need to take responsibility for your own dive. You also need to be aware that you may even have to come to the assistance of your experienced buddy if they get something wrong or get into difficulty. Mandy's buddy was a veteran diver. Luckily he was in good physical shape so was able to make the long swim back once they had been carried out to sea. If he had not been so fit, Mandy might have had to tow him to shore.

Start diving the right way by

taking responsibility.

12. Becoming a Diver WILL Change Your Life

At some point after you have finished your course, there is a very good chance that you may undergo a transformation. At first, you are merely someone who has learned how to scuba dive. But, one day you may wake up and realise that you have become a diver.

Scuba diving may not occupy your every waking thought but, when you are not under water, you will find yourself spending a lot of your time working out when, where and how you can arrange to be under water again, and soon. You will join diver chat rooms online, seeking out like-minded folk to exchange views with and ask advice. You will complain that your old friends just don't seem to understand you any more. You start identifying yourself as a diver and you start to hear others referring to you as a diver too. You have become hooked by the transformative experience of leaving the chaotic surface world and escaping into the peace of the ocean depths, entranced by wonderful new sights and relaxed by the meditative sounds of your own breathing. You have caught "the bug!"

This is what diver Anne has to say about the experience.

"Five years ago, I learned to dive. Now, I have stopped counting my dives but the number is over 400, for sure. I envy people who still keep logging their dives, though. I wish I had the discipline. Five years ago, I never expected that I would be an underwater photographer and videographer, would win prizes, get interviewed by dive magazines and publish my own book of photographs. Five years ago, I never thought I would one day be able to hold my breath for over a minute and pose as an underwater model in a mermaid outfit."

"Five years ago, I did not expect that my painting would become influenced by my underwater adventures and I would be an Ocean Artist. Five years ago, I never imagined that diving would introduce me to places in my own country, Indonesia, that I had never even heard of. Nor did I expect to find so many great new friends who share my interest in the ocean. In the past five years, many of my habits have changed. I buy more bikinis than dresses. My body lotion now has a sun protection factor and I wear flip-flops rather than high heels. Instead of clubbing, I now go to beach parties. And the gossip does not revolve around fashionistas and fabrics; it's more about fish and fins."

"How will my life evolve in the next five years? I cannot wait to find out!"

Anne is not alone. Becoming a diver will change your life and not only if you discover the sport when you are young, as she is.

Jan, a pharmacist, was 57 years old when she learned to swim. At the age of 62 she took her first scuba diving course. She sold her business, retired and decided to go diving. She is now in her mid-seventies and has logged over 2,000 dives. She is an accomplished underwater photographer and an expert on coral reefs and their inhabitants.

In his thirties and in possession of both a career and a mortgage, Simon, a Suit (with a capital S) in the City of London met Andrina, who was working as a dive master on a remote Caribbean island. Three years later, she convinced him to move out there with her and they embarked together on a journey around the world, working in a variety of jobs in the scuba diving industry. This is a journey that still continues today, 12 years later. Simon often speculates how life would have turned out if he had not joined a dive club when he was at university. None of the scenarios he comes up with sound anywhere near as much fun as what he has actually done.

Life Changes

Ask any diver and they will tell you how the sport has changed their life; and always for the better.

You make new friends, from much wider social circles than before and from all over the world. Scuba diving is an excellent equaliser and breaks down social, financial, language and cultural barriers that otherwise separate people. When you are on a dive boat, you are a diver, the same as everyone else. It does not matter how old you are or how wealthy you are, where you come from or who you are.

You dress almost identically, you share similar experiences and, underwater, everyone looks the same. Everyone learns to dive the same way, everyone encounters and overcomes the same challenges; everybody follows the same learning curve. So when you meet another diver for the first time, you already have much in common. A bond already exists between you.

The fact that divers come from all walks of life means that it is normal for many divers only to meet in diver-to-diver scenarios; at the club, in the dive centre, on the boat or on the beach. If you do happen to encounter each other in other aspects of your daily life, maybe when you serve one of your dive buddies a drink in the bar you work in or when you pick them up in your taxi, it can seem strange at first. Here is someone whom you know extremely well, but the context is alien. Sometimes it even takes you a while to realise who they are. An oft-repeated phrase is, "I didn't recognise you with your clothes on!"

You will have fun: maybe more fun than you thought you could have. Diving will take you back to your youth. A diver will come up from an hour underwater, hair all over the place and with a glob of snot hanging from the left nostril. They will remove their regulator, spit phlegm into the ocean then look at you with the biggest smile you have ever seen and scream, "Woo Hoo!" And the grin on your face will be as wide as theirs, because you know exactly what they mean.

Divers are not cool. They are not competitive; they are not insular. They don't worry about what other divers think of them. They share their joy unreservedly. No matter how adult and aloof you may have trained yourself to be in your working world; once you are on a dive boat, the fun-child in you will emerge. Every dive you do with a group is followed by a bout of often-raucous sharing. A diving friend named Tracy calls this "jabber." The better the dive, the higher the "jabber" factor, as everyone banters back and forth about what they have seen and done.

On a more sombre note, be prepared for your attitude towards certain things to change. Your awareness of the environment, the depredations of the human race and the damage we are wreaking on our planet will be raised substantially. Divers see the consequences at first hand. You will find yourself at times diving among bits of floating plastic and other non-degradable trash. You will swim over reefs that are beige, silty and dead because of coastal over-development. You will visit places where there used to be many big fish but they are now all gone.

These things will anger you and you will feel the urge to do something about it all. Many divers are active and vocal advocates for change in human attitudes towards our environment. They make responsible seafood choices. They consider their carbon footprint. They respect animal life. To quote a common but apt cliché, when they interact with the ocean "they take only photos and leave only bubbles."

Scuba diving is a sport and will give you some exercise, but be warned, the better a diver you become, the less exercise you will get. This is because, with experience, you learn to slow down, move less and let the ocean do much of the work. Diving plus sea air plus camaraderie equate to an appetite. So it is not unusual for divers to actually gain weight, the more they dive. Be wary of this. Fit divers are better divers. Excess fat can make you more tolerant of cool water but it can also make you more susceptible to decompression illness. Scuba diving may actually give you a reason to go to the gym more often, rather than less.

Your spending habits will change. Diving opens up a new world of new toys as well as new places to go. Areas you had never previously heard of will leap to the top of your travel must-go list; places like Raja Ampat, Anilao, Komodo, Scapa, Silfra, Sudan, Bikini, Truk, Yap or Palau. The world will suddenly seem a much bigger place, especially as a good chunk of the planet below the water is now accessible.

Dive travel is different. Adventurous diver Cindy describes it thus.

"Spending 42 hours getting to your destination is not unreasonable if the diving is worth it. Dive equipment takes priority over clothing when you pack. Flight plans are juggled around nitrogen loading. Wardrobe choices revolve around wetsuit thickness rather than evening wear. Land footwear is dive booties or flip-flops. There's no room for anything else."

"Your carry-on bag is full of regulators, computers and cameras as these are the things you can't live without. Your check-in bag smells of wet neoprene. You know that, wherever they come from, the only other out-of-towners sitting in the waiting room of airports with names like Mingankabau will speak the language of divers and you will get on famously despite not sharing a mutual language.

You don't have holidays any more: you have wonderful, glorious, amazing, wild, epic adventures."

Buddies for Life

It is wise to anticipate the effect that these substantial life changes can have on your relationship with your partner. I mentioned the exotic new destinations that you will plan to visit. As a diver, your focus will be completely on the diving and what you will see underwater. Many wonderful dive destinations are very beautiful topside too, but, in most cases, there is very little for a non-diver to do.

Strongly consider learning to dive with your partner, not necessarily together but around the same time. You may find it strange that I do not automatically assume that, if you and your partner both want to dive, you will join the same course. Why wouldn't you? Well, the decision is completely up to you but one thing all instructors learn early on is that teaching couples together can be a pain in the neck.

In the chapter *Twelve Ways You Can Help Your Instructor* I mentioned the phenomenon of couples bringing their unhelpful relationship habits to class. Some couples tend to compete with each other when stressed and confronted by challenges and this does not make for a calm, positive learning environment. Be honest with yourselves when considering whether you should learn to dive together or apart. The end result, that you both become good divers, is the important thing.

I should add a further caveat. If you have a partner who is already a diver, please dissuade them from trying to have anything to do with your training, no matter how experienced they are. The instructors and their assistants do not need any help and enthusiastic amateurs just get in the way.

Is it impossible for a diver and a non-diver to maintain a healthy, long-lasting relationship? Of course not! Former pharmacist Jan, who I mentioned earlier, has a non-diving husband, whose passion is racing vintage cars. Every time she goes off diving; he buys a new set of wheels.

But for Simon and Andrina, the couple who met in the Caribbean, scuba diving forms the framework of their life together. As for Anne, who has shaken off her high heels; she is still single but go back and see what she says about how diving has changed her and guess how likely it is that her eventual life-partner will be a diver too.

Start diving the right way by

being prepared for the fact that it will change your life.

13. Aspects of Etiquette

In every sphere of human activity there are conventions that govern the behaviour of the participants. These may not necessarily be set in stone or legally required and enforced. Sometimes they just become established and generally accepted over time. Scuba diving is no exception.

When you first start diving, it is very likely that you will be among the least experienced divers in any group. There is no way of hiding your inexperience and there is no need. All divers were in your position once and most will be sympathetic and ready to help and advise. Don't pretend to be more knowledgeable than you are. Watch carefully how the more experienced divers behave. Copy what they do and when they do it. Don't be afraid to ask questions, particularly about boat rules. Not all dive operations have the same procedures and when you are diving with any operator, the etiquette is to follow their way of doing things. Listen closely to briefings and be prepared to be flexible.

Divers are often very free with advice for new divers on how to behave. Sometimes this will be helpful. On other occasions, they may simply be giving vent to pet peeves that are actually just personal preferences, rather than aspects of universal diver etiquette. Many have strong opinions, bordering on obsession, about things that really don't matter in the larger scheme of things, for instance whether it is OK to pee in your wetsuit or whether you should wear a snorkel when you dive. In this chapter, I discuss matters of etiquette that are genuinely important, either on safety grounds or to ensure that your acceptance by the community of divers proceeds as smoothly and quickly as possible.

However, as I mentioned the issues of peeing and snorkels just now, I should not leave you hanging. A phenomenon called immersion diuresis makes people want to pee when their bodies are subjected to pressure underwater. If you pee in your wetsuit, it will make your wetsuit smell until you rinse it out. Also, if you submit to the urge to pee early on during a dive, it is very likely that you will feel the need to pee several times more. If you can resist the urge, so much the better. However, as dehydration is a major contributory factor to decompression illness, it is very important to drink plenty of water both before and after a dive. Don't ever avoid drinking water before a dive just so that you do not have to pee.

The same thing applies as far as stress is concerned. Stress is dangerous because it can lead to panic and diver stress is usually created by multiple minor factors. So, if holding back the urge to pee on a dive is causing you stress, it is far better to let it all out, rather than have it prey on your mind. If you do pee, try to flush your wetsuit out a little when you are back on the surface and before you get out of the water. Or use the deck shower if there is one. If you still smell a bit, don't worry about it. You won't be the only one.

As for whether you should dive with a snorkel; well, sometimes you should and sometimes you don't need to. If you think there is a chance, however remote, that the dive may require a long surface swim, then you take a snorkel with you. If you are sure there will be no long surface swim under any circumstances, then don't take one. If you don't know or are not sure, take a snorkel anyway.

Dive Boat Etiquette

Make sure the day before the trip that your dive gear is working and that you have packed both everything you need and nothing you DON'T need. Arrive early and ready to go. Departing on time is often crucial to the success of a trip so, if you are late, the boat will often leave without you, even if you have booked and paid in advance. And, if it does wait for you, your tardiness will not endear you to either the crew or your fellow travellers.

On day boats, space is often very limited so pack with care, using a gear bag or a small plastic crate. Pack your scuba gear in reverse order of use; i.e. the things you will need to get out first should be at the top. Stow your gear neatly out of the way and keep everything together both before and after the dive.

Keep your phone and cash in a dry bag in the dry area but keep your scuba spares box with your dive gear rather than in your dry bag, as there is every chance you will be in your wetsuit when you need it.

Keep out of designated dry areas if you are wet, even if you have a damp towel around you. On any boat, never leave a cylinder standing unsupported. They are heavy, metal objects and a falling cylinder can crush a toe, destroy a regulator second stage, crack a mask or demolish a dive computer as well as cause irrevocable damage to the cylinder valve.

For similar reasons, keep weight belts in a box or on the deck and out of the way. Never put a loaded weight belt on the bench beside you or anywhere else where the movement of the boat could cause it to fall.

Keep your own most fragile pieces of gear, your mask and dive computer, in crush –proof boxes in your dive bag when you are not using them. They are the two things most likely to go mysteriously missing on a dive deck, get smashed by a wayward scuba cylinder or fly off the side of the boat and into the water. So, once you have your wetsuit on, take your mask out of your dive bag and slip it over your neck. Then grab your computer and fit it securely on your wrist. Always make sure either that you are wearing both your mask and computer or that they are both in their boxes in your dive bag. They should never be anywhere else.

Watch your divemasters as you are on your way to the dive site, and, when they start to put their wetsuits on, you do the same. They are anticipating and making sure they are ready to do all the things they have to do when they arrive. You do not have as much to take care of as they do but, as a new diver, it may take you more time than the others to put your equipment on, so it is good idea to get ahead of the game.

Entry and Exit

On most dive boats, you attach your BCD and regulator to the cylinder before the boat gets moving but you only put the equipment on just before you get in the water. In this case, your more experienced companions are your guide, rather than the professionals, who will often need to gear up before you so they can check water conditions at the site.

Once you have all your equipment on and it is your turn to head for the entry point the correct thing to do is move directly but with caution. You have a large object strapped to your back so it is a little more difficult to squeeze yourself through small spaces. Etiquette is all about being considerate. Take extra care when standing up and sitting down; be aware that the person next to you might choose the exact moment you stand up, to bend and strap on a fin. They will not take kindly to encountering the swinging tail of your cylinder with the side of their head. I have seen countless near misses in my time, as well as many hits!

Remember two basic rules: "look behind you" and "avoid sudden movements." Once you are in the water, move away from the entry area so others can enter safely, then unite with your buddy or group before you descend.

When returning to the boat, exercise ladder courtesy. Wait your turn; never hang below someone climbing the ladder in case they lose their grip and fall. Exit the water quickly then move away from the area directly above the ladder so others can follow you.

Rinse Tanks

There are fresh water tanks on most boats so that divers can rinse the salt water off camera equipment, computers, dive lights, masks and other bits and pieces. Often there will be two tanks, one for camera equipment and one for everything else.

The two most important things to remember about rinse tanks are: -

1. Don't place anything in a rinse tank unless you are completely sure exactly what the rinse tank is for.

2. Don't ever leave anything in a rinse tank; just dunk it to remove the salt water; then take it out and put it in a safe place.

Beach Etiquette

Not all dives are done from boats, although most aspects of good boat diving behaviour obviously apply on shore as well. From an etiquette point of view, the main difference between boat diving and shore diving is that there are more non-divers around, so you need to keep their feelings in mind too. Don't park your vehicle where you may obstruct someone, as you will not be available to move it while you are underwater. Keep noise to a minimum, especially after night dives, when whooshing valves and clanging cylinders can disturb local residents. Keep your equipment organised as you would on a boat. Having a large purpose-built beach mat for setting everything out and gearing up on is a good idea. If there is a bathroom nearby, use it. Most importantly, leave no litter behind.

Nudity

Diving involves changing clothing, which can obviously involve temporary nudity. One of the great things about our sport is that it brings together people from different backgrounds, walks of life and cultures. But some of these folk may not have your broad-minded attitude to public exposure or share your own high opinion of the beauty of your naked form. For the comfort of all, therefore, good etiquette requires discretion when you dress and undress.

Seasickness

The toilet on a boat is called the "head". This is not because it is where you should put your head if you feel seasick. The best place to hang your head is over the side of the boat, preferably the side where the wind will carry away the contents of your stomach when they appear. Your fellow travellers will appreciate it as will the crewmember whose responsibility it is to clean and unclog the head. The fish under the boat will be happy too at the unexpected delivery of manna from heaven.

Environmental Etiquette

I mentioned previously that divers as a community tend to be more deeply concerned about the environment than the general public and are particularly sensitive to the preservation of the ocean. Many divers do not eat certain types of seafood and are very protective of fish and corals: indeed, marine life as a whole.

Etiquette demands therefore that, not only do you comport yourself underwater so that you don't damage anything but that you are also aware of other threats to the reef too and do not contribute to these. Many sunscreens have been identified as containing chemicals that kill corals so, rather than lathering up, protect yourself from the sun by wearing a dive skin or a rash guard and shorts, as well as a hat or a hood. Make sure any sunscreen you do use on your face and hands does not contain the preservatives and UV filters that have been cited as harmful to marine life.

Nose Etiquette

A final personal etiquette tip concerning post-dive snot: if your buddy emerges from a dive with their face smeared with nose debris, point it out to them subtly with a smile. Fortunately, etiquette does not require you to offer to wipe it off for them.

Lost Dive Gear

It is an established convention that an item of dive equipment found under water should be returned to its rightful owner. To benefit from this community-friendly piece of etiquette, make sure that you tape your email address or phone number to anything you think you might drop in the ocean, such as your mask, camera, torch or dive computer. If you come across something that someone has lost, make every effort to locate the owner. After all, what goes around comes around.

Animal Etiquette

The convention is look but do not touch! This does not just mean big animals like turtles, manta rays and whale sharks; it applies to the smaller animals too. In fact, you could argue, the smaller an animal is, the more vulnerable it is.

Some operators prohibit their divers from wearing gloves in an effort to discourage them from laying their hands on the reef and its occupants. There is much debate over whether a glove ban works and it is an issue that can arouse strong feelings. I believe that educating divers is more effective than imposing rules. I do not think that most of the people who wear gloves do so because they want to interfere with the marine life. Gloves can make you feel more comfortable or help keep you warmer. Nor do I believe that someone who wants to disturb the animals is going to be dissuaded if they have to do it with bare hands. However, good etiquette also requires that if you want to dive with an operation, you abide by its rules.

Underwater

If one of your companions points something out on a dive or calls you over to show you something they have found, it is good etiquette to show appreciation with an OK signal and spend a few seconds studying it before moving on, even if what they have shown you is something you have seen a million times before. Having said this, as a new diver, control the urge to point out everything you see to your buddies until you have enough experience to distinguish the rare from the everyday. Unless, of course, you are pretty sure that you have spotted something significant, in which case it is worth taking the risk. After the dive, you really do not want to be the only one on the boat who saw the six-gill shark or the psychedelic frogfish and didn't show anyone!

If you are in a group and the guide points something out, be aware of where your fellow divers are before you charge over to see whatever it is. It is courteous to invite other divers to look first but if they demur and insist that you go ahead, say thank you with an OK sign. Take a look, just long enough to post the cool animal onto your memory wall, then move out of the way.

If you are diving with photographers and you see them busy with a subject, it is not done to intrude; either to take a peek at what they have got in their sights or to crack off a quick snap on your own point-and-shoot.

Photographers also need to be considerate, however, particularly if what they are photographing is something unusual. Good etiquette dictates that a diver without a camera has just as much right as a photographer to see, watch and examine an animal. So if you are taking pictures, take them promptly, then leave. If you want to come back to the animal, you can re-join the holding pattern and wait until everyone else is done.

It is in circumstances such as these that the swimming, positioning and manoeuvring techniques you learned in class become very important. When you are in close proximity to other divers and when the animal that everyone wants to see is on or close to a sandy seabed, it is vital that you control your arms and fins. So keep your arms tucked in and concentrate on what your fins are doing and where they are, particularly when you are moving away from the viewing area. A careless kick could mess up the visibility for everyone that follows you, or worse, send some rare marine creature flying off into oblivion.

While I am on the subject of flailing limbs, despite exercising every care and attention, you may inadvertently catch a kick in the face from a fellow diver. The etiquette is to act as if nothing happened, while making a private note to keep a little further away from your assailant in future. You certainly shouldn't refer to it once you are both back on the boat. They already feel bad for having caught you and, after all, one day it will be you who inadvertently whacks one of your fellow divers in the head and you will be very pleased if they don't mention it!

Returning to the topic of photographers, the convention is to steer well clear of them, unless they specifically invite you to pose for a photo. Be aware of the effect your positioning in the water might have on what the photographer is working on. For instance, if you pass by carelessly up current from a photographer, the debris of your passage might drift into their shot. If you swim below a photographer working on a reef wall and exhale just after you pass, you will send a snowstorm of expanding and exploding bubbles into their meticulously framed backdrop.

If you are diving as part of a group, it is poor etiquette and potentially unsafe to go off on your own or exceed the depth and / or time limits specified in the briefing or agreed before the dive. Your divemaster has planned the dive based on a set itinerary. If you depart from that, you place the group at risk. If you do not like the way the group dives, then choose another group or dive operation in future. There are many dive boats and dive centres that allow experienced dive teams to set their own dive plans and run their own dives. But when you dive with a group, you stay with the group.

Which reminds me: a final tip. Study the other divers in your group at the start of the dive. Look at what they are wearing and memorize their appearance. Yours may not be the only group on the dive site and you want to avoid making the same embarrassing mistake that countless divers before you have made; that of somehow switching groups during the dive and ending up surfacing at the wrong boat! Not only do you have to suffer the humiliation of being returned red-faced to your original boat, but your "disappearance" might have caused your original group to raise the alarm and report you as missing.

Start diving the right way by

being aware of the etiquette.

§4

Your First 20 Dives

14. What's Next?

You have received your first scuba certification card. Your instructor has shaken you warmly by the hand, you and your fellow students have celebrated your achievement and you have posted the news on line and told the world. You are a diver!

Well, yes you are. But, not to diminish your achievement, you are a diver in the same way that someone who has just passed their driving test is a driver.

So, what's next? The best advice I can give you is to go straight off and do another course, then do some supervised fun diving.

You may have been told that your first scuba certification qualifies you to go diving in the company of a similarly experienced person without supervision. Well, technically it does. But the truth is that no beginner's course these days is sufficiently all-encompassing that it will arm you with all the information, skills and in-water experience that you need to become an independent, capable diver.

The course will have taught you how the equipment works, how to rescue yourself from the most common emergencies that may take place and how to work together with another diver. It will not have taught you how to assess conditions at a dive site and plan a dive, how to find your way under water or how to deal with fast currents, limited visibility, dark water or deep water.

These things were not omitted because they are unimportant. They are very important. Nor is it the case that you did not learn them because your instructor was negligent or unprofessional. It is just that there is only enough time in a beginner's course for a new diver to assimilate a limited amount of information. You acquire enough skills and information to keep you safe in relatively shallow water, when conditions are benign and you are diving as part of a supervised team. Your first course brings you to the point where you are comfortable enough with the basics that you can now focus on more complex aspects of scuba diving.

Anyone who tells you differently is misleading you. After completion of your first course, your mind set should not be: "that's it, I've done it; I'm a diver now; I'm ready for anything." It should instead be, "ok, I'm pleased with what I have achieved but there is evidently much more to mastering this sport and I need to learn more."

So, as soon as you complete your first course, sign up for the second. Most agencies describe the next training level as "advanced", although it's really just "post-basic."

The Advanced Diver Course

An advanced course will give you five or six further dives under an instructor's direct supervision, in a variety of conditions or circumstances. This widens your experience considerably. It does not turn you into an expert overnight, but there is no question that this course does help you progress far beyond beginner standards.

A good advanced course should include a night dive, at least one dive deeper than those you did on your first course, a dive where you learn underwater navigation techniques and two or three further dives. All these dives should have three key aims: teach you some new things, give you plenty of swimming time and offer you lots of opportunity to perfect the neutral buoyancy skills you learned on your beginner's course. With the possible exception of the deep dive, all should be good, long dives. You should expect to get a minimum of four hours underwater during the course.

A significant additional benefit of taking the course is that you can dive deeper. Many dive operations, following their training agency rules, require evidence that you have completed an advanced diver course before they will allow you to join a dive where the target depth is below 18m (60 ft.)

The price of the advanced course usually includes the use of standard dive equipment and dive and boat fees, so, when you compare the cost with the price of fun diving, it is usually not that much more expensive. When you do a course, no matter what else you learn, you also get the additional benefit of spending quality time in the water with someone who is paid and perfectly placed to give you constructive criticism on all aspects of your diving, as well as answer your questions. So this is your chance to ask about all the things you wish you had asked about on your first course.

Night Diving

Many instructors do not like running a night dive as part of the advanced course because it gives them a longer day and interferes with their social life. This is understandable as they do work very long hours, usually for relatively poor financial rewards, and are not paid by the clock.

But a lot of people love night diving and you might like it too, so you really should insist on including a night dive in your course, as it is best to do your first night dive under instructor supervision. It will not only calm any all-too-natural concerns you may have about diving in the dark. You will also learn a number of skills that are not necessarily intuitive but are nevertheless essential for safe, pleasurable night diving. You will learn light etiquette, how to signal, how to ascend and descend safely in the dark, how to navigate at night and how to move close to the seabed. Night diving is not so complicated that you need to take a full course on it; one dive on your advanced course should be enough to show you how it is done and give you the taste for more. Maybe afterwards, you can buy your instructor a refreshing post-dive beverage to say thank you for working overtime?

Your First Fun Dives

By the time you graduate from your advanced course, you will be much more capable and confident than you were when you took your first few breaths underwater only a few dives previously. Will you be ready to dive anywhere in any circumstances? No. Some dive sites, even very well known places, require a substantial amount of experience. Some dive sites feature conditions, such as extreme depth, cold, moving water or an overhead environment like a cave or a wreck, that may put you in a situation where you do not have the skills to manage the dive safely. When this happens you are not in control of the dive. We refer to this as being "beyond your comfort zone."

The problem is that when you begin diving, you do not know where your comfort zone is until you find yourself outside it. Here is a story that illustrates the point perfectly. Robert, an experienced diver, was sitting quietly at home one afternoon, when he received a call from a lady who introduced herself as a friend of a friend. She asked him for advice on which dive operator she and her husband should go with if they wanted to dive at Nusa Penida. This is an island off the south coast of Bali, famous for big fish, but also notorious for deep, cool water and strong, unpredictable currents that make it an accident black spot.

Robert asked about their experience and the lady told him that she and her husband had only learned to dive a few weeks earlier. On hearing this, Robert pointed out that diving around Nusa Penida could be tricky and he suggested that they try instead some of the wonderful diving in easier conditions off the village of Tulamben on Bali's north east coast. The lady was highly indignant at what she saw as Robert's implication that she and her husband were "not excellent divers; which we are" and hung up on him.

Two days later, the lady called Robert back to tell him that she and her husband had gone to Nusa Penida and that they had had a perfectly wonderful day's diving. "So there, everything you were telling me was wrong," she said. Robert just told her he was glad she and her husband had enjoyed their dives.

The point here is that Robert was not wrong. Many people who go to dive off Nusa Penida have a great time and their day is completely uneventful. However, the water conditions there can combine to make a dive very difficult and dangerous for new divers. Many people have come to grief there.

Robert was not saying that everyone who dives at Nusa Penida comes to harm or gets lost at sea. All he meant was that conditions there can put new divers in difficulty and that there are other terrific dive sites on Bali where conditions are more benign and where new divers will not be taken outside their comfort zone.

The lady evidently did not understand this. She and her husband were probably unaware of the concept of a comfort zone and the fact that some dive sites, even popular ones, are inherently more dangerous than others. The lady seemed to have misunderstood that, having learned to scuba dive, she was now capable of diving anywhere. She was so convinced of this that, when a local expert advised her to go diving somewhere else; rather than listen to him, instead she took offence at his well-meaning advice. Maybe he should have explained further what he meant. Maybe the lady did not give him an opportunity.

As I said, Robert was right. There is no reason for new divers to choose places like Nusa Penida when they can go instead to other sites that offer equally excellent diving but less risk. They can put more challenging dives on their "to-do list" for the future, to consider when they have more experience.

It is not just a question of someone getting hurt. Many new divers have an experience that takes them out of their comfort zone and scares them, but they survive it unscathed. Unfortunately, the incident shakes them so badly that their reaction is to conclude that scuba diving is not for them and give up the sport completely. This is such a waste and so unnecessary! If new divers start off with straightforward dives before progressing to more difficult dives, they are much more likely to keep diving and continue to enjoy this wonderful sport for their whole life.

Your Comfort Zone

So, how can you avoid making the same mistake as Robert's "friends of friends?" How can you know where the edge of your comfort zone lies? You may find out where it is once you go outside it but how can you perceive the frontier from inside your comfort zone? Let me try to help.

For a new diver who starts diving by doing the first two courses consecutively, as I recommend, your comfort zone for your first 20 dives is a dive where these factors apply.

1. The water is no colder than the water you did your training dives in.

2. The depth is no deeper than the maximum depth you dived to in class.

3. The visibility is no worse than the visibility you experienced in your training.

4. You can see the reef, wall or seabed from the surface.

5. Your planned ascent route at the end of the dive is marked by a line going from the seabed to the surface or by a reef wall that goes up to the surface or very close to it. If you have a visual reference it is much easier to manage a safe, slow ascent: and

6. You are wearing similar equipment to the equipment you used on your training dives.

Your first 20 dives should NOT include sites where: -

1. You will go inside a cave or shipwreck or under ice.

2. You will be dropping on to a dive site you cannot see from the surface.

3. Your planned ascent route is in blue (or green) water where you have no visual reference.

4. You are likely to be buffeted by strong currents that can sweep you off the dive site, such as you might find on a mid-ocean pinnacle.

Unfortunately dive sites do not come with difficulty ratings. Maybe they should? In snow skiing, slopes have colour ratings according to their difficulty. For instance green slopes are for beginners and black slopes are for experts. This makes it easy for skiers to select the slopes that suit their ability or experience.

There is no such system in scuba diving. You have to do your own research. Some dive operations have their own rules for divers wanting to visit particular sites. Many have a checkout dive system, which enables them to assess divers before they decide which sites they will take them to.

Checkout Dives

If a dive operation does not know you, they may ask you to make an initial dive in relatively shallow and calm water before taking you to more challenging sites. This is called a checkout dive. They will do this no matter what certification card you produced when you booked with them. A card is only evidence that you once did a training course. It does not provide proof of ability.

Many sport divers have busy lives and dive only when they are on vacation. This means they often have long gaps between dives and, during this down time, their skills get rusty and their instincts and memories fade. An up-to-date logbook is a better indicator of a diver's true level but nothing beats seeing the diver actually in the water.

The checkout dive allows the operation to see how skilled you really are, correct minor issues and make sure that the sites you are taken to match your competence. It also gives you a chance to get used to your equipment again and reacquaint yourself with the underwater world in easy conditions.

You will often be asked to practise basic mask and regulator skills during the dive. If the checkout dive points up significant skill deficiencies, you may be assigned to an instructor or divemaster to work on these before you go out diving again.

Rescue Diver Training

Once you have around 20 dives under your weightbelt, you should be feeling confident enough in your skills and comfortable enough in the water to be able to focus at least some of your attention on what other divers are doing around you.

If this is the case, it's time for Rescue Diver training.

This course teaches you how to manage stress in yourself, identify signs of stress in others and help another diver in an emergency. In short, it transforms you from a diver whose only interest is their own survival into a considerate member of a diving team. Many divers find this the most rewarding of all classes and, in the right hands, it can be something of a watershed. This is the point at which many people decide that they will be divers for life.

Start diving the right way by

knowing what to do next.

15. It's not Always About the Cards

D iver training agencies are commercial businesses and would like you to believe that the only way to develop your scuba knowledge and skills is to sign up for one of their vast array of courses. While time spent with an instructor is indeed a very good way to improve your technique, you do have other options.

More Than Just a Guide

A few months ago, I joined a dive liveaboard charter and found that two of my fellow guests were very new divers, with 4 and 24 lifetime dives respectively. We were in Raja Ampat in Eastern Indonesia, where the diving is fabulous, the corals are lush and the fish life is as plentiful as anywhere in the world. It is also a patch of ocean where currents can be intense. A number of the best dive sites can be tricky if the conditions are not perfect, which is rarely the case. So Raja Ampat is not really the right place for beginners.

This liveaboard usually attracts experienced divers and there are no instructors on board, only dive guides, whose job it is to make sure the divers get the best possible dive at each site by leading them along the optimum route and spotting marine life as they go along.

One of the dive guides was placed in charge of the two new divers on the checkout dive on day one. As soon as he saw how new they really were, he made it his mission to do his utmost to teach them how to be better divers.

He taught them how to weight themselves correctly and how to descend properly. He showed them how to make a slow, safe ascent with a safety stop and how to raise a surface marker buoy from their safety stop to show the tender boat where they were. He also showed them how to swim against a current and how to use a reef hook to stay in place when a current is running.

He taught them to swim horizontally and efficiently, using a variety of fin kicks, and how to remain motionless in the water, so they could observe marine life up close and take pictures of it. (Of course, despite their lack of experience, both divers had cameras.) On deep dives he reminded them to concentrate and not get distracted and made sure they monitored their computers even more frequently than usual. He also briefed them and guided them on their first night dive, which they loved!

By the end of the week, the two divers were transformed. They were comfortably accomplishing dives in a high current that even veteran divers were shying away from. They were working together as a team and becoming less dependent on the guide with every dive.

Did they receive a diver certification card at the end of the week? No! Did they become better divers? Unquestionably! Did the guide feel a sense of considerable pride in what he had achieved? Absolutely! Will the new divers recommend the guide and his operation to friends and the dive community at large? Every time!

This was a perfect example of how excellent diver training does not always need to be about reading assignments, quiz completion and card collecting.

The success of the week, of course, was not solely down to the efforts of the dive guide. It was also due considerably to the students' willingness to learn. While you are fun diving with professionals, do not be afraid to seek advice on equipment, technique or how to manage certain diving environments. You just have to pick a moment when they are not busy with other things and ask.

They will always be ready to help and will usually be very pleased you asked. It is much better to have divers in your charge who confess they do not know something and want to learn, rather than deal with folk who are unwilling to admit ignorance, pretend to know everything and then get themselves into difficulty.

Clubs and Classes

In the world of yoga, aficionados regularly attend classes led by an instructor. They are taken through a variety of positions, shown how the positions should be performed, gently advised on how they might improve next time and, of course, praised fulsomely when progress is made. The classes keep the students active, enthusiastically involved in the sport and yoga fit.

As a diver, try to follow a similar programme to stay dive fit. No matter how experienced we are, most of us become better divers during a dive vacation and, by the end of it, swimming on scuba is as natural as walking. After a few months out of the water, however, polished instincts become dulled and acute skills become less sharp. So, by the time we come to the next dive trip, we find we have to climb the learning curve again before we are back at our optimum level. It is no coincidence that, wherever people dive, the largest number of accidents take place at the beginning of the diving season.

Even if you choose not to learn to dive with a local club, you can still join one after you are certified. The club may be affiliated with a particular training agency or it may operate as part of a private or community sports centre. It may have been established by an enterprising and enlightened urban dive centre or by an independent local instructor. Whatever its structure and background, it will keep you actively diving all year round. As part of its regular programme, the club will run skill circuits in a swimming pool and organise local dives at weekends.

As well as the additional practical experience they offer, these activities allow veteran divers and instructors to mingle with newer folk on an informal and social basis, so information and advice can be exchanged and assistance provided with skills and technique. Like yoga classes, no cards are handed out and the cost is usually very affordable. Volunteer-managed clubs have low overheads and the professionals don't run the sessions at a profit. After all, it is in their commercial interest to keep people involved in the sport. Active divers buy more equipment and join more dive trips.

If you can't find a club in your town or area, then think about establishing one of your own and recruiting some locally-based divers to join you. If you need a further incentive to take the initiative, you might be interested to hear that, as well as enabling you to keep your diving skills sharp and enjoy social opportunities with like-minded folk, a dive club also gives you buying power. Dive resorts and liveaboards will often offer advantageous deals for group bookings. So you can keep dive fit, hang out with scuba people and get cheaper dive vacations too!

Start diving the right way by

knowing that it is not always about the cards.

16. Taking Pictures

It used to be the case that instructors would advise new divers not to bring cameras underwater on their first few dives because taking photos would distract them from the things they should be concentrating on, such as controlling their buoyancy, remembering to check how much air they had left and making sure they stayed in touch with the group.

This is still very good advice. New divers genuinely need to focus completely on their diving technique to stay safe. Getting distracted by taking pictures can compromise a new diver's safety.

However, these days, trying to persuade someone not to take a picture or video recording device of some sort underwater, no matter how much experience they have, is as futile as asking the sun not to shine. For many of us, the primary reason for doing anything, and certainly for doing anything as ultra cool as scuba diving, is to share it on social media. Our smart phones and pocket digital cameras are with us 24 hours a day, every day, so we certainly want to carry them with us when we learn to dive. And we will not be impressed by anyone who tries to stop us.

So, instructors and dive operators have to adapt to the times and balance safety with the need to meet the requirements of their customers, while always keeping safety considerations paramount, of course. The dive centre you learn with may arrange for one of its staff to take pictures and video of you during the course, so you just have to concern yourself with the diving. Or, you may be allowed to take a camera with you during your course but you will only be permitted to use it at certain specific times.

After you graduate and become a certified diver, of course, the decision on whether you take a camera with you when you dive is up to you. This chapter assumes that you will not be able to resist!

Electronics and Sea Water Do not Mix

There is a basic problem with taking anything that has electronic parts into the ocean. If the electronics come into contact with sea water the device will be destroyed, forever. Once you are below the surface, the pressure of the surrounding water is greater than the air pressure inside your device, which means the seawater is always actively trying to get in.

Some cameras are waterproof to a certain depth and that depth is usually marked clearly on the casing. The vulnerable electronics inside are protected by one or more rubber o-rings that seal all potential water-entry points.

If your camera or phone is not at all waterproof, or not to the depth you are planning to dive, then it has to be carried in a dedicated waterproof box, called a housing. Housings are depth rated too but most are usable to normal sport diving depths, 40m (132ft) or shallower. The housing shields the device from the water, again with the help of rubber seals. It is designed so that you can still activate the camera controls when it is in the housing. Each housing is custom-designed for a specific model or family of devices.

All underwater photographers know that it is not a question of "if" an o-ring will fail, it is a question of "when." One day, the o-ring will break or get displaced, or a hair or piece of fluff will break the seal, and the high-pressure water you are swimming through will get in. The water never stops trying to get in and one day it will succeed. A flooded camera or phone cannot be fixed.

So have your device insured. Oh yes, and download your photos after EVERY dive. I have a friend who once spent a two-week trip-of–a-lifetime taking incredible pictures, only to have his camera flood on the last dive. He had not bothered to download any of the images he had shot and lost an entire fortnight of unrepeatable memories.

Hands Free

Experienced underwater photographers use big camera systems that they have to keep in their hands throughout the entire dive. They have a tether, which they use to attach the system to their BCD in the event that they ever have to let go of it completely, but this is rarely required. Over time, they have acquired highly developed control skills that allow them to dive virtually hands free. As a beginner, you do not have these skills. You may acquire them some day, but it will take time and a lot of diving. For now, you need your hands for a variety of important things: for instance: to adjust your BCD, equalise your ears, check your air or clear your mask. This means that your first underwater camera or housing should be small enough to be stored in a BCD pocket when you are not taking pictures, leaving your hands completely free.

Remember too that you will be moving about a lot during a typical dive. Most of the time you will be horizontal; at times you will be vertical. Some of the time you may even be upside down or lying on your back. So there is a good chance that anything you put in your pocket will fall out, unless the pocket is zippered or completely velcro-ed shut.

Even if the pocket is tightly closed, one thing every diver finds out very quickly is that when you take something out of a pocket underwater, everything else in the pocket comes out too. So, like everything else you put in a pocket and do not want to lose, your camera needs to be secured to your BCD harness by a lanyard. This is a piece of cord long enough to allow you to take the camera out, use it without detaching the cord and put it back. Always make sure that the cord goes back into the pocket too and does not just float around in the water waiting to get snagged on to something.

Taking Bad Pictures

Your first underwater photos will certainly impress any non-diving friends and relatives but they will not satisfy you: for two reasons.

First, any selfies you take, or pictures you have taken of you, will not show the svelte, streamlined, mermaid or merman you imagine yourself to be. You will look awkward and ungainly, your hair will be everywhere and your mask-framed eyes will look huge. Your lips around the mouthpiece of your regulator will make you look like the victim of a bad Botox operation, your arms and legs will be stuck out at bizarre angles and your equipment will probably look like it is trying to escape from you.

The second reason you will not be satisfied is that your photos will not reflect the amazing things you see underwater. They will be blurry and everything will have the same dull blue-green colour. Your marine life pictures will mostly consist of disappearing fishtails and those fish you do capture in full will look much smaller and less interesting than you remember.

A huge step towards solving the first problem is to listen to your instructors, watch what they do and follow their lead. Cinch down straps, tuck loose ends away and attach hoses securely to your harness. Use proper fin-strokes. Don't just flap your feet around aimlessly. Concentrate on keeping your arms and hands close to your body.

You may notice that this advice reflects techniques I describe In the next chapter, "Ten Tips for Reducing Your Air Consumption. These techniques will not only give you longer dives, they will also make you a more relaxed, controlled and aware diver. As a side benefit they will also improve how you look when you dive and make you much more photogenic.

On the topic of modelling tips: if you have float-away hair, tie it up, braid it or wear a hood. Also, avoid staring face-on into the lens when you pose for photos. Look away from the camera, preferably at something else in the frame.

Taking Good Pictures

Which brings me to the question of how to fix the second problem. Good underwater photographs do not just happen automatically; you have to learn how to take them. The best way to do this is to take a class with an underwater photographer. There are a number of simple tips and tricks that the pros know and that are easy to learn and apply, no matter what device you are using. You will not be taking magazine quality pictures, of course. It takes many years of experience to develop the know-how to reach that level. However, the leap in quality between the photos you took before the class and those you take afterwards will astonish you.

A good underwater photography course can also do wonders for your diving skills. It will improve your buoyancy control and help you towards that nirvana of being able to remain motionless in the water. After all, if you are unbalanced and unstable, you will not be able to take clear, sharp pictures.

A caveat: not every dive professional who has an Underwater Photography Instructor badge is an underwater photographer. Most training agencies have a system which permits instructors to self-certify as "specialty" instructors and there are those whose qualification to teach the course derives just from having read the manual before you did. Choose an instructor with a proven track record. Look at photos the instructor has taken, check their social media profile or ask to look at a portfolio. Get them to prove themselves. After all, that is what you would ask of anyone offering you services in any other walk of life.

Start diving the right way by

taking photos but not losing sight of the bigger picture of dive safety.

17. Ten Tips for Reducing Your Air Consumption

O nce you have completed your first course and begin diving with more experienced divers, one of the first things you may notice is how much longer their air seems to last in comparison to yours. You are always running low before the rest of the group and having to cut short your buddy's dive.

The people who dive with you will not mind at all. They know you are a new diver and it was not so long ago that they were in a similar situation. However, you probably WILL mind and you will be looking for ways to breathe more efficiently and make your dives last longer.

Here are 10 tips guaranteed to improve your air consumption as well as make you a better diver in many other ways. Notice that none involves using a bigger cylinder!

Tip One – Get in the Mood

Take some quiet time on your own before each dive to relax and focus on what lies ahead. Breathe deeply and find a nice peaceful place in your mind. Put away any negative thoughts concerning other aspects of your life. You are going diving. There is nothing you can do about anything else while you are underwater.

Tip Two – Breathe Properly

Learn to breathe like a diver. Breathe from the diaphragm; push your stomach out to allow your lungs to expand and draw in as much air as possible. Then breathe out long and slow, bringing your stomach in to reduce your lung volume to a minimum. Practise this long, deep, slow breathing cycle until it becomes instinctive. Not only will this help you to use less air, it will help you stay calm and think clearly.

Tip Three – Get Fit

Diving is a sport and the fitter you are, the less air you will use. Start a programme of aerobic training and increase the level of your training as a dive trip approaches.

Tip Four - Don't Move Unnecessarily

When you are underwater, only move your fins when you need to go somewhere. If you are not going anywhere, keep them still. Tuck your arms in, only use your hands if you need to signal and incline your body like a motorcyclist if you want to change direction or regain your equilibrium.

Tip Five – Remove Weight

Like many new divers, there is a good chance that you are wearing too much weight. A reliable indicator of this is if, after your initial descent, you have to add quite a lot of air to your BCD to keep you off the bottom. What happens next is that, when you start to swim, the air in your BCD lifts your upper torso and the weight around your middle drags your butt and legs down. This gives you the head up, tail down posture of a seahorse. Look at other new divers or ask a friend to take a short video of you, to see what I mean. Moving through water in this position takes much more effort and causes you to use up much more air than if you are horizontal, as you should be.

The trick is to reduce the amount of weight you are carrying. Start by removing one piece and, if you can still make a comfortable initial descent by exhaling fully as you leave the surface, remove another. If, at the end of a dive, you can hang at a depth of 3 to 6m (10 to 20ft) with 50 Bar (750 psi) in your cylinder and an empty BCD, you are correctly weighted. Another little thing to remember: if you are wearing a weightbelt and a wetsuit, the belt will loosen and slip down your hips a little as the water pressure compresses your suit. So, once you are at depth, take a moment to hitch your weightbelt higher on your waist and tighten it a little. This will lift your legs up and give you a more horizontal posture in the water.

Tip Six – Do an In-Water Check

The whole gearing up, entry and descent process can be awkward and strenuous. For instance, you may be wearing a thick suit on a hot sunny day, there may be a lot of other divers around or the sea might be choppy. A whole host of factors can conspire to undo the positive effects of your pre-dive relaxation and the consequent stress can cause you to go through your air more quickly. So, once you are underwater and the confusion on the surface is behind you, make it a habit to pause briefly and go through a quick in-water check. Take a few seconds to compose yourself, get your slow, deep breathing cycle going, inspect your gear for problems and verify your cylinder pressure before heading off for the depths.

If all this does not work and you can't shake off your anxiety then don't just carry on with the dive feeling stressed. Signal to your buddy and guide, ascend slowly, get positively buoyant on the surface and swim back to the boat. Everyone has days when it just doesn't feel right.

Tip Seven – Kick Differently

There are much easier ways to fin than the classic wide, full-legged scissor kick you learned in your beginner's class. Use alternatives like the frog kicks and modified flutter kicks that I describe in the chapter "Snorkelling Dos and Don'ts." If you don't fully understand my descriptions, watch your instructors and dive guides and copy what they do. Using energy-saving fin techniques will reduce your air consumption considerably.

Tip Eight – Know your True Starting Pressure

The cylinder pressure you see when you check your gauge on a sunny boat deck is misleading. The cylinder is hot so the air inside is hot and the heat causes the pressure reading to rise a little. The reading will fall again once you enter the relatively cool water and this underwater reading is your true starting pressure. Once you know this, you can calculate your airtime and this will help you relax. A relaxed diver uses less air.

Tip Nine – Always Know How Much Air You Have

Always know how much air you have left and also have at least a rough idea in your mind of how long it is going to last. This is how you do it.

A Metric Example

As you descend, make a mental note of your air pressure, say 190 Bar.

After five minutes at depth, look again. Maybe you now have 170 Bar.

This means you have used 20 Bar, in five minutes

Assuming you are diving the deepest part of your dive first, you now know that you will use a maximum of 20 Bar every five minutes.

If you want to surface with 50 Bar, you have 120 Bar left to use.

So a simple calculation ((120 / 20) x 5 minutes) tells you that you have AT LEAST 30 minutes of airtime left.

An Imperial Example

As you descend, make a mental note of your air pressure, say 2900 psi

After five minutes at depth, look again. Maybe you now have 2700 psi.

This means you have used 200 psi in five minutes.

Assuming you are diving the deepest part of your dive first, you now know that you will use a maximum of 200 psi every five minutes.

If you want to surface with 500 psi, you have 2200 psi left to use.

So a simple calculation ((2200 / 200) x 5 minutes) tells you that you have AT LEAST 55 minutes of airtime left.

Tip Ten – Keep Calm

If you ever find yourself becoming anxious underwater, the chances are that this is because you have lost your deep, slow breathing cycle without noticing it. Maybe you have been fighting a current or trying to keep up with a buddy who is swimming at a pace that you are uncomfortable with.

As soon as you are aware of your increasing anxiety, stop finning. Calm yourself down by inhaling fully and, most importantly, exhaling fully for a couple of minutes. As you take deeper and gradually less frequent breaths your mind will clear. Check your contents gauge. If you still have plenty of air left, continue with your dive. If your air supply is lower than you expected, ascend to a shallower depth. Remember, the shallower you are the less air you use.

Start diving the right way by

learning to breathe efficiently.

§5

Staying Safe

18. Beating the Cold

A couple of years ago, a diver named Irene wrote to me for advice in advance of a trip she was planning around the island of Alor in Eastern Indonesia. I told her about the sites and currents, the fish she would see and a couple of land tours she should do. I also told her that, in the southern part of the straits, water temperatures could be as low as 18C (64F) and suggested she take a thick wetsuit and a hooded vest with her.

A few weeks later I saw that Irene had posted in social media that she had enjoyed her trip but complained that she had only taken a thin wetsuit with her and the water in some places had been "freezing." She said she had been so cold that she had been unable to concentrate, that she had experienced a couple of anxious episodes and had cut short some of her dives.

I messaged her, reminding her that I had told her that it was likely that she would encounter cool water and she replied telling me that I had been right. "However," she added, " after you wrote to me, I looked online at all the pictures people had posted of their trips to Alor and it all looked so tropical and sunny that I didn't believe you!"

Warm Up Top: Cold Below

If you learn to dive in places where lakes and seas are cool, the topic of keeping warm when the water and air temperature are on the chilly side will be an important part of your course. Your instructors will cover in detail the clothing, the equipment and the physical, physiological and psychological factors involved in cool water diving.

The reason why I dedicate a Scuba Fundamental chapter to this topic is that, when you learn to dive in tropical waters, these issues are rarely even mentioned. However, even if you have no plans ever to dive outside the tropics, cool water conditions are still a factor you will sometimes need to consider. Just because air temperatures are high and the sun is shining does not mean that the water is warm.

As anyone will know who has ever visited Bali's Nusa Penida in the summer months, looking for the elusive, exotic mola-mola, tropical seas can become very cold at certain times of the year. In Horseshoe Bay in the south of the Komodo Straits, divers have even been known to wear dry suits to stay warm and comfortable. In winter in Egypt, the swimming pools are rarely heated and the water temperature can be as low as 14C (57F.) This can come as a surprise when the pool looks out onto a desert landscape baking under blue skies. It is not a pleasant surprise either, particularly if you have chosen to learn to dive there to escape from colder waters at home in Europe.

As Irene discovered, holiday photos do not show how cold the water is and many divers go to places like South Komodo or the Galapagos Islands unaware and under-prepared. They only find out what is in store for them when they back roll in and gasp with shock as the cold hits them. If you are accustomed to diving in warm waters and are not physically and psychologically ready for lower temperatures, not only can diving in cooler water be uncomfortable, it can pose a threat to your safety too.

It is very important to stay warm on a dive primarily because an insidious phenomenon known as progressive hypothermia can lead to a diver becoming confused and disorientated.

The Warning Signs

Shivering is the most obvious sign that the cold is having an effect on you. When you shiver, it is a sign that your body is desperately attempting to generate heat by increasing your metabolic activity.

Physically you may start to feel stiff or develop cramps. Mentally, although you may not feel uncomfortable, the cold can gradually take your attention away from the things you should be concentrating on, such as navigation and monitoring your dive time and air supply.

Your ability to reason becomes impaired, which can lead you to make poor decisions. You may also forget routine procedures, especially if these have been poorly learned and insufficiently practised, and this could cause to you to react too slowly or do the wrong thing in an emergency.

Prevention

Knowing how and where the body loses heat and dressing to combat the threat of hypothermia are the first steps in your survival strategy.

You lose body heat from four principal areas: your head, neck, thorax and abdomen. So these are the places you need to protect by wearing a thicker wetsuit or by adding a neoprene vest or two. Make sure one of the vests has a hood attached.

Some people find it difficult to get used to wearing a hood so, before adding one to your diving equipment for cold ocean dives, it is best to try wearing one in a pool first so you can get accustomed to it in relatively benign circumstances. You may find it uncomfortable or restricting at first, but it is worth persevering with it, as hoods are such effective insulators.

A couple of tips: don't wear your mask over your hood. Put the mask on first then pull your hood up and over the strap. If the hood does not already have a hole in the top, make a hole there so any air you exhale that subsequently finds its way into your hood can escape and does not start creating a big air bubble on top of your head.

Who is most at risk?

When you are exposed to cold, your body concentrates on protecting its core temperature and this means reducing the flow of warm blood to your extremities. People with more fat are more resistant to hypothermia because it takes longer for the cold to penetrate to their core. If you are slim, you are more at risk, so take greater precautions.

What to do

During a dive in cool water, if you begin to feel unusual aches and pains; if your thoughts are starting to concentrate more on the cold and less on the marine life or if you realize you have lost track of your depth, time and air supply, signal your companions and abort the dive immediately. Do not wait until you start to shiver. Ascend slowly, establish surface buoyancy and waste no time in making your way back to the boat or shore directly and purposefully.

After you are back in the dry, remove your wetsuit and vest immediately as, although neoprene offers insulation from the cold underwater, when it is wet and you are on land, it has the reverse effect. Instead of making you warmer, it will draw heat away from your body. While you are warming up, make sure you have someone around to monitor your wellbeing as reheating your extremities can cause your core body temperature to fall.

Start diving the right way by

dressing to beat the cold and recognizing the danger signals.

19. Surface Safety

The Dive centre chartered a boat to take five divers and two instructors out to some islands off the south coast of Bali. It was rainy season and, behind the rainclouds, there would be a full moon that night in an area where currents are notoriously strong and unpredictable. However, water conditions seemed manageable, there were other dive boats out on the water and, having done one dive without encountering any difficulties, the divers entered the water again for a second dive that was to be a drift dive.

After about 10 minutes underwater, they found that the current was so strong that it was difficult to keep the group together so they ascended early to find that a storm had swept in, surface conditions were now very rough and the rain had reduced visibility to a few metres / a few feet only.

Unaware that the divers had surfaced and expecting that the dive would last an hour or so, the boat crew did not pull up their anchor until about 40 minutes after the divers had entered the water. They moved off to look for them in the area they expected them to be. They did not find them. They could not search for long, as they were low on fuel. Then night fell and the divers were gone.

A little over 72 hours later, searchers found four of the divers perched on rocks some 20 kilometres (12.5 miles) away from their original entry point and one of the instructors in the water nearby. The bodies of the remaining diver and the other instructor washed up on shore in the following days.

This was not a bizarre one-in-a-million accident. Indeed, it is just the latest in a depressingly similar series of such incidents that have taken place in recent years.

Just before midnight on 7th July 2012, a fishing boat picked up eight divers adrift in 3m (10ft) seas off southern Bali. The divers had begun their third dive of the day late in the afternoon in rough water. They had been caught by a strong current, become separated from their guide and had surfaced out of sight of their dive boat. The boat was then forced to return to port after a very brief search because it did not have night-running lights.

The divers were 30 kilometres (18.5 miles) from their starting point when the fishermen spotted lights in the water. Their rescue was completely fortuitous. In fact, the captain of the fishing vessel said that normally if he saw a light in the water at night he would think it was another vessel and steer away from it! He had not been looking for them. He was just on his way home. An official search had been planned but it was not due to begin until dawn!

It was not only luck that turned what could have been a screaming headline into a mere footnote. The divers contributed to their own survival by making two crucial decisions. First, they stayed together, creating a larger, more visible presence in the water and enabling each to take mental strength from the presence of the others. Second, some of the divers were carrying flashlights, even though the dive had started during daylight.

These two factors turned the odds sufficiently in their favour to enable them to benefit from the chance encounter with the fishing boat and survive.

Prevention and Precautions

Similar stories abound everywhere people dive and there are strong currents. This is one of the reasons why many divers fear drift diving. Which is a shame, because dives when a current is running can be the best dives of your life. Current attracts and galvanises marine life, especially larger fish, and this translates into action and excitement. There is actually no need at all to be afraid of currents or drift diving. Incidents such as those I describe in this chapter are completely avoidable as long as you AND the people you pay to take you diving adopt some basic procedures.

What You Can Do

The first thing to do to reduce the risk of being lost at sea is always choose a professional dive operator who knows the area well. However, no matter how good the operation seems to be, you too must share responsibility for your safety by taking your own precautions.

On any dive, there is always the chance that, when you surface, the pick up boat will not be close by. It may not even be in sight. Don't automatically assume that something is wrong and get anxious. This does not necessarily mean that they have lost you or left you behind. The boat may just be busy collecting other divers who have become detached from the group and have surfaced elsewhere. But you cannot assume that, when they do come to look for you, the crew will immediately see your small head amid the vastness of the ocean. You have to give them a little help to find you as quickly as possible. Here are a few things you should do.

1. Always carry an inflatable safety sausage / delayed surface marker buoy. Make this a permanent part of your dive gear and never leave it behind. Choose tall and thin and orange, yellow or pink. Pick up crews all over the world have told me that they see orange safety sausages first. Some published surveys say yellow is more visible. Whatever colour it is, a glossy white flash on the top will reflect sunlight and make you even more visible.

There are also alternative "here-I-am" signalling devices on the market. I know a diver who carries a yellow flag wrapped around an extendable and collapsible pole, secured to the bottom of her BCD harness. Recently, a kickstarter company was looking for funding to develop a system that consisted mainly of a brightly coloured helium balloon kite attached to a length of cable.

2. Have something on you that makes noise, such as a whistle or, better, a power horn attached to your BCD inflator hose. Sound can carry a long way, especially down wind, and bring you to the attention of searchers who may not have seen your safety sausage.

3. Carry a dive light on every dive. As I mentioned in the second story earlier, it can be a lifesaver. It is also very useful to have a light with you when you are looking for shy marine life like lobsters, rays or eels hiding under rocks and ledges.

4. Consider wearing a hood when you dive. Not only will it keep you warm underwater, it will also protect you from the sun if you are ever left drifting for any length of time. A glossy, white, reflective flash on the hood will make you easier to see.

As well as carrying equipment to help searchers find you, you can reduce the risk of getting lost at sea by doing a few things that may seem to be common sense but are often forgotten.

1. Especially on a drift dive, stay with the group and don't head off on your own. Several divers together on the surface are MUCH easier to spot than one or two.

2. If you are diving from a boat where you are a stranger, introduce yourself to the crew and make sure they remember you. Don't be the "invisible" diver who gets forgotten.

3. Don't do drift dives when the sea is very choppy, on a rainy day or misty day when surface visibility is poor and searchers may have difficulty finding you.

4. Make it a rule to do late afternoon dives only in the same sort of location as you would do a night dive, such as in a protected bay where there is little water movement.

How to Choose

In each of the stories I told above, the people responsible for putting the divers in the water and looking after them made some major mistakes. These were not disasters caused by random chance or some freakish event. They were borne of ignorance and neglect. Unfortunately, the fact that a dive operator takes your money does not mean that they are professional. Every business that runs scuba diving will tell you that safety is always their number one concern, but sadly, in many instances, this is simply not the case. So you have to exercise a substantial degree of judgement when you choose who will take you diving.

Do as much research as you can. Investigate each dive operator's safety record. Ask for feedback in scuba diver online forums. Check the previous history of the location too. Many places, even well known and popular dive sites, are notorious accident black spots and, if you plan to dive one of these, you should be even more cautious than normal. As I advised in the chapter "What's Next?", such locations are better left on your to-do list until you have more experience.

Never hesitate to walk away or sit out a dive if you think your operator is being careless, does not seem properly prepared or equipped or you just feel that something is wrong. A diver wrote to me recently following a frightening dive day she and her friend had experienced at the hands of a very unprofessional outfit in Mauritius.

One problem after another culminated in her being left floating alone in the ocean for a long time. She realised afterwards that she should have known what was in store from the moment the crew came to pick up the dive bags from the hotel room and left one bag behind. In retrospect, she said, that was the point at which they should have cancelled and found another operator.

Ask questions. Never worry what people will think of you. Never assume that just because the more experienced divers in your group are not asking questions, that everything is therefore OK. For example, if the boat you are doing a drift dive from has only one engine, ask what the back-up plan is if the engine fails. If it is a larger boat with many divers, ask what the system is for making sure all divers are back on board after a dive. If you don't like the answers to your questions, don't dive.

Particularly with drift dives, make sure that your dive operator has a plan for the dive, including emergency procedures if bad weather intervenes or if the in-water dive guide decides to end the dive early. Make sure that there is a staff member on board whose job it is to make sure the dive boat follows the divers and to work with the in-water dive guide. Ideally, look for a dive operator that uses VHF radios, locator beacons or similar devices in waterproof housings to help the boat staff and the in-water dive guide communicate with each other.

If it Happens

If it ever happens that you are left on the surface for more than a few minutes, make yourself as buoyant as possible. Keep your signalling devices deployed and, if you have any difficulty at all keeping your head above the waves, drop your weights (but retain your weight belt, see below). Leave your mask in place, to stop sea water from going up your nose, and keep your gloves and hood on, so that you stay as warm as possible. If you are wearing a dry suit, put some more air in it.

Tie yourself and other divers together with weight belts and BCD straps. It is easy to drift apart and hard to resume contact once you have become separated. If you see the shore is close, swim in that direction, cutting diagonally across any current there may be, rather than fighting it directly. Most importantly, keep your spirits up and don't lose hope. Wherever you are in the world, searchers will come who know how to follow currents.

The Value of Expertise

A few years ago, I was part of a group on a morning dive. A couple of hours later, after lunch, one of the divers realised belatedly that he had lost his camera. He guessed he had dropped it while he was climbing back on to the boat and hadn't noticed. The camera was in a housing that was positively buoyant so he did not think it had sunk. Two members of the crew took a speed boat, returned to the spot where the divers had been picked up and then followed the current lines as they coursed around a small group of islands and out to sea. After two hours, they came across the camera. The housing it was in was a small, clear, transparent box floating in an enormous expanse of clear transparent water, but they still found it.

What is the lesson to take away from this story? Surface survival rule number one. Dive with experts!

Start diving the right way by

Knowing how to keep safe on the surface.

20. Where's the Oxygen?

A couple of years ago I joined a day boat for one of its regular weekend dive trips. The plan was to go to a group of offshore islands for the day. We had just tied up to the mooring and were getting ready to dive when our attention was drawn by a burst of frenetic activity on a larger dive boat close by. A wet-suited figure was being manhandled out of the water and onto the stern of the boat. We first thought that this might be a training exercise, but soon realised from the serious expression on everyone's face that we were looking at a genuine emergency. A diver was in trouble.

The captain was shouting from the wheelhouse at other divers floating in the water and telling them to get back on board fast. Meanwhile, the wet-suited figure, completely inert, was laid out on deck by two crewmen, who then squatted down next to the figure, apparently checking for life signs. Everyone else on board had moved towards the cabin amidships and they were all standing there, faces pale and transfixed on what was going on at the stern. The captain called over and asked if we had any oxygen. We did and handed over our big green oxygen kit as the boats met bow to bow. With a nod of thanks, the captain turned his vessel round and headed off at full speed for the mainland, a good 45 minutes rough ride away.

We never found out if the injured diver survived nor what had caused the accident, but we all knew that the combination of cool water, fast current and considerable depth at the edge of this bay had, in the past, caused more than a few inexperienced divers to panic and elect for a rapid ascent as a way of "just getting out of there!"

The Wrong Choice

When a diver is injured following a rapid ascent, or when a diver conducts a normal ascent but subsequently reports symptoms that could signify decompression illness (DCI), there is a standard procedure to follow. Briefly, you give the injured person first aid, then, assuming they are still alive, administer 100% oxygen via a tight-sealing mask over the mouth and nose.

An injured diver should be given oxygen as quickly as possible and delivery should continue until the oxygen supply is exhausted or until a diving doctor instructs that it should be stopped. For this reason, every responsible dive operation, whether boat or land-based, should carry a sufficient supply to allow a diver with suspected DCI to continue breathing oxygen until they arrive at a medical facility with oxygen on tap. The dive operation should also ensure that at least one member of staff on every dive trip, is qualified in first aid and oxygen administration.

The diver in this incident had unfortunately chosen to dive from a boat that was carrying no oxygen at all. Luckily for the crew, and for the diver I hope, we were in the right place at the right time and were suitably equipped to help.

An Important Question

Before you dive with any operation, no matter how apparently professional it seems, make sure they have an appropriate answer to the question, "Where's the oxygen?" Whether it is a dive from a beach or boat, the daily briefing should cover the key issues of where the oxygen is and who among the staff is qualified to deliver it.

Sadly, many operations are ill-prepared and under-equipped to deal with a diving emergency and the oxygen issue is often glossed over or not mentioned at all. This is not always an oversight. They may actually have no fixed plan to deal with a case of DCI, using the dubious rationale of "it hardly ever happens so it is not worth thinking about until it does."

Some dive centres, those that don't bother to have oxygen and oxygen delivery systems on hand when they run dive trips, may even instruct their staff to tell you that oxygen is not really that important. This is a lie. Nobody who has had any sort of professional diver training actually believes this. You can be sure that, if they were ever to have a diving accident, they would get on oxygen as fast as they could.

The quick administration of oxygen after a diving accident can make an enormous difference to the injured diver's subsequent quality of life. It can even be the key factor governing the diver's survival.

Failing to Plan

However, even top dive businesses are guilty of failing to plan adequately for emergencies. For example, liveaboard operations always carry oxygen on board the mother-boat but rarely on the small tenders that ferry divers to and from the dive sites. Often this ferrying involves long rides to allow the mother-boat to float free in the deep channel away from the reefs. This means that if a diver blows to the surface, the nearest oxygen is a long way away and, as I said earlier, any delay in delivery can have a crucial impact on whether the diver lives.

Neither is the presence of an oxygen kit on a dive boat always a reliable indicator that the dive operation is prepared to deal with an injured diver. Given that accidents that require immediate delivery of oxygen are thankfully rare, the equipment can sit for a long time without being deployed. Stories abound in the dive industry of boat crews turning to the kit in an emergency and finding that the unforgiving marine environment has caused the rubber hoses to waste away and corroded the cylinder valve to the point of immobility.

So, if your question, "Where's the oxygen?" is just greeted with a vague gesture in the direction of the green box, followed by a quick change of subject, you are right to be suspicious. By all means press the issue and ask them to show you the equipment and tell you who among the team is qualified to deliver the oxygen. After all, as a diver you have a vested interest in ensuring that the people you are paying to take you diving are taking their responsibilities seriously. The prospect of a few awkward questions might just encourage the idle or negligent to get their act together!

Start diving the right way by

knowing where the oxygen is.

21. Look Out Below

Marna was a new diver and her first proper dive trip was to the Cayman Islands. One day, she went to a site where the dive guide said there was a huge grouper that really liked eating sardines and Cheez Whiz. So all the divers were given some to take down with them to feed the grouper. The grouper emerged from its cave in the reef and Marna held out some of the sardines for it to eat but kept the rest in her other hand behind her back, wanting to save them to feed to other fish that were milling about.

The grouper moved away and Marna was kneeling on the sand, watching all the action, when she felt something behind her engulf the hand that was still holding the sardines and slowly work its way up her lower arm. It was the grouper, which had sneaked up and had sucked half her arm into its mouth. Marna let go of the sardines and pulled her arm out. She swears her fist made a popping sound as it emerged from the grouper's fat lips. Her heart beating like a drum, she swam away as fast as she could and made a promise to herself never to get involved with any fish-feeding activity again, just in case this sort of thing happened again and the fish started feeding on her instead of the fish food!

One of the most common reasons quoted by non-divers when asked why they don't dive is that they are afraid of being attacked by dangerous sea creatures. Marna's experience hardly constitutes an attack but diving will often bring you into contact with fish and other marine animals whose size, teeth or temperament can pose a risk. In this chapter I quote a few more examples. Note that, in most of these instances, divers have done something to engage (or enrage) the fish in the first place. The primary message to take away from this chapter is not that the ocean is a dangerous place, but "Yes, there are things in the ocean that can hurt you but, if you respect them and don't disturb them, they will leave you alone."

Thin Sharks and Fat Sharks

As I said right at the beginning of Scuba Fundamental, sharks pose very little threat to scuba divers. A good general guideline though is "thin sharks good, fat sharks bad." Most of the sharks you see on the reef, the skinny white tips and black tips that lie on the sand or cruise around looking for slow-moving small fry, are much more scared of you than you are of them. Even the more curious grey reef sharks are more like inquisitive puppies than threatening wolves.

The fat sharks that come in out of the blue, such as oceanic white-tips, bull sharks and tiger sharks, are the ones that you want to avoid. These guys are scared of nothing and the wise thing to do if you see one is to stay close to the reef or seabed and keep your eye on it as it cruises by. It will usually ignore you and act as if you are completely beneath its contempt.

Divers who post pictures on social media of themselves in the water with fat sharks have usually participated in shark feeding dives, where sharks are attracted to a particular site at a set time of day by someone dropping bucket loads of fish oil, blood and dead and dying fish into the water. Once the sharks have arrived, they add a few divers to the soup.

As was the case with Marna's grouper, the sharks have no way of understanding how they are supposed to behave at such gatherings and occasionally there are stories of divers getting hurt. Generally speaking, however, there is little risk involved. The sharks are just interested in the food and, if they bite anything else, it is entirely accidental. Often the victims are the divers running the show, who just get their timing wrong or forget to let go of the bait. The best operations endeavour to make the event as natural as possible and surround the experience with education designed to increase awareness of how shark populations around the world are under threat.

Much debate exists over the ethics of shark feeding, indeed fish-feeding in general. There is no question that it is entertaining, even thrilling. The doubts revolve around whether it causes the fish to acquire new behaviour that ultimately threatens their survival and whether the activity is always truly as educational as its proponents claim. There is also the issue of collateral damage. Reef fish are caught to feed the stars of the show and the reef itself can suffer, with excited divers resting on it either to avoid or film the action and sharks thrashing about in the coral to retrieve chunks of bait that have fallen into a crevice.

Other shark-bites-man or woman stories involve the most peaceful, innocuous sharks you can imagine. Bottom-dwellers like nurse sharks and wobbegongs will lie motionless under rocks and in caves ignoring the divers that gather to watch and photograph them. Unfortunately, for some people, just seeing the shark is not enough. Like the small boy running a stick along the bars of the cage of a sleeping lion, they want some action. They want to see the shark "DO something." So they will pull its tail or poke it with a pointer stick and that, of course, is when these normally docile fish will react. Particularly, if they have the misfortune to live at a relatively busy dive site and they find themselves being constantly provoked.

Naturally, afterwards, the shocked divers will claim that they were not doing anything and that the dangerous man-eating shark just attacked them for no reason. They have a story and scars that should make them the centre of attention at dinner parties for years to come. And each time they tell the tale, they drive another nail into the coffin of sharks as a species. It is unfair to classify an animal as dangerous if they are just responding instinctively to a perceived threat.

Titan Triggerfish

Sofia was a divemaster working in the Red Sea when she had a "Titanic" encounter. She takes up the story. "The boat was moored over a sandy bottom just off the reef where we had been exploring. I was swimming back to the mooring line when I felt a stabbing pain in my upper leg. I had no idea what it was. I turned around to see what had happened and saw a titan triggerfish swimming away. It swung around and came charging back towards me, evidently returning for a second bite. I turned onto my back to keep my eyes on the fish and position my fins between it and me. I got to the surface in no time, without bothering to do a safety stop. I had no wish to spend 3 minutes fighting off the aquatic equivalent of a pit-bull terrier.

Back on the boat, I took off BOTH my wetsuits: I was wearing a full 7mm wetsuit over a 3mm shorty. And I found that I had a set of tooth marks in my leg. The Titan had managed to leave tooth marks through TEN millimetres of neoprene. There was no bleeding but within an hour there was a massive black bruise about 10cms (4 ins) around. Over the following few days it turned every colour of the rainbow but even when the bruise had gone I was left with a dent in my leg, probably muscle damage, that is still there 15 years later. The other divers with me had also been attacked but fortunately they had seen the Titan attack me first. So they saw the threat and had time get their fins in the way. All they had to compare were tooth marks in rubber."

Titan triggerfish are some of the most aggressive fish in the sea, especially when they are protecting eggs in the hollow nests they build in the sand. They have extremely strong jaws and can deliver a powerful bite, which makes them well worthy of mention here! If you ever see a Titan muscling its way towards you at speed, move out of the danger zone swiftly. This means swimming away from the nest laterally rather than ascending, as the Titan's protective area extends above the nest too. In the chapter " Six Essentials" I mentioned a number of things you can use your fins for. Here is another one. You can use your fins to protect more vulnerable parts of your equipment and anatomy from a titan triggerfish's jaws. Use them either to create a "wall" between you and your assailant, as Sofia's divers did. Or use power strokes to propel you away from the danger area as fast as possible.

These fish are not to be toyed with. They have no sense of humour. I once watched a diver on a safety stop try to attract a titan triggerfish by pulling a frankfurter sausage out of his BCD and waving it in the water. When the fish swam in to take it, the diver pulled the sausage out of the way at the last moment. The titan turned round and the diver held the sausage out again, teasing it to have a second try. I groaned to myself, knowing what was coming next. The titan came muscling in with its usual fast, swaggering swimming motion but this time it ignored the sausage completely and went straight for the diver's face, hitting him with the full force of its jaws right on the forehead. A cloud of green blood obscured the diver's head completely and the Titan barrel-rolled away in victory. I'll say it again. They have no sense of humour.

Lionfish, Scorpionfish, Stonefish

Some of the other fish you really need to be wary of are a little smaller but exceptionally well camouflaged. Scorpionfish, stonefish and lionfish all belong to the same family and have venomous spines along their back. The lionfish is the easiest of the three to spot as it suspends itself above the reef, disguised as a patch of floating weed, waiting to pounce on its prey. The scorpionfish and stonefish also use concealment as their strategy, the scorpionfish blending indistinguishably with the colours of a coral reef or wall, the stonefish hiding invisibly among grey and brown rocks and dead coral fragments on the seabed.

The secret to avoid being harmed by any of these camouflaged killers is good buoyancy control. Almost every lionfish / stonefish / scorpionfish accident I have ever heard of involved a diver flailing an arm around or putting a hand down on a rock that was not a rock, in a nervous and misguided attempt to stay stable in the water. This is yet another powerful reason for you to work hard on mastering the "Six Essentials."

If you do get stung you will feel immediate pain. There will usually be a lot of swelling and the skin around the wound will turn purple or black. Nausea, vomiting, shock, respiratory arrest or even cardiac arrest can ensue so you will need the help of an attentive buddy.

Barracuda and Needlefish

Barracuda are hard to spot as their streamlined bodies reflect the colour of the water around them. This makes them hard to photograph too. They operate in the open ocean away from the reef, usually in the shallows where the sun's rays penetrate the water and glint off the scales of their prey. Adult fish are usually solitary; the juveniles move around in schools. When a barracuda decides to strike, it is all over in an instant. One moment the barracuda is just hanging there, apparently bored, then the head and tail of a snapper are suddenly floating separate in the water and there is chaos on the reef as every fish reacts. You look for the barracuda again and it is back exactly where it was, looking unconcerned and gulping down the centre section of its victim.

Barracuda are opportunistic hunters and have been known to attack divers, although not with malicious intent. A piece of jewellery hanging around a diver's neck and catching the sun can produce the same flashing effect as the glint of white scales as a struggling fish turns belly up. The flash can attract a barracuda's attention and cause it to react automatically. It is therefore a good idea to leave your chains, pendants and necklaces at home or in the hotel safe when you go diving.

Needlefish, especially the larger crocodile needlefish, are often mistaken for barracuda although they are quite different and seen side by side you would never confuse them. They have long sharp pointed beaks, live near the surface and present a very different threat to divers; a threat that you cannot really do much about. I was on a liveaboard once and saw a group return from a night dive looking as if they had been in a warzone. All were bleeding from puncture wounds in the head, chest or arms. They had been on the surface waiting for the boat to come and pick them up when a school of needlefish had "attacked" them.

In over 30 years of diving I had never heard of anything like it but I did a little research and it turns out that this type of incident is not at all rare. Needlefish have a habit of making short jumps out of the water, perhaps to escape predators. They swim fast and very close to the surface and will often leap over the decks of low boats rather than go around or under them. This jumping activity seems to be encouraged by artificial light at night and stories abound of night fishermen and divers being "attacked" by excited needlefish speeding across the water towards their lights and crashing into them. Apparently, for Pacific Ocean islanders who often fish on reefs from low boats, needlefish represent a greater risk of injury than any other fish.

What can you do? If you ever see a school of needlefish as you ascend from a night dive, reduce the number of light sources your group shows on the surface to the bare minimum and hope they ignore you.

Moray Eels

Jim had done a number of dives, during which his guide had entertained him and his buddies by enticing moray eels out of their lair with food. Jim thought this was pretty cool so, when he took a new girlfriend out diving one afternoon, just the two of them on a diving date, he decided to impress her with a similar trick. Having forgotten to bring food with him, he improvised by fluttering his fingers in front of the hole where the moray eel lived. His plan was to attract the moray's interest, then move his hand well out of reach once it had appeared. His strategy worked. The moray eel emerged and Jim was delighted. He turned to make sure that his girlfriend was as impressed with his skills as he was, but misguidedly left his fingers fluttering near the hole unsupervised. He felt excruciating pain and turned back to see the moray completely out of its hole, its mouth clamped firmly onto his hand. Now he definitely had his girlfriend's attention!

Moray eels are ambush predators and have large mouths and backward-facing teeth to ensure that prey, once caught, cannot escape without further damaging itself. The fish they usually feed on move fast, so in order to catch these fish, moray eels need to be able to move even faster. They are thought to have poor eyesight. This moray's vision was evidently good enough to spot Jim's fingers but not good enough to identify that they were not food. To this day, Jim has no idea how they did it but eventually he and his girlfriend managed to get the moray eel to release his hand and he made it to the surface and to the hospital treatment room without too much blood loss. He did lose his little finger, though.

Moray eels may look angry but their habit of opening and closing their large toothy mouth is not a display of aggression. It is just a convenient way of directing water over its gills so it can breathe. Left alone, they are entirely benign and make great photo subjects.

Some dive guides and instructors use unnatural interaction with fish to entertain customers. Don't copy them. Just because they are professionals does not mean that everything they do is necessarily "professional." There are many things that instructors and divemasters do that do not set a good example to divers. In fact, in my book Scuba Confidential, I devote an entire chapter to the topic.

Sea Snakes

Morays are long and slender but they are eels, not snakes. A number of species of sea snake inhabit the tropical waters of the Pacific and Indian Oceans. They are highly venomous but shy of divers and not at all aggressive. Although they live their entire lives in the sea, they have to surface in order to breathe so you will often spot them as they are coming up or going back down again.

Diver mythology would have you believe that one reason that sea snakes are not a threat to divers is that their mouths are very small and could not even encompass a finger. Therefore the only place a sea snake could ever bite you would be on the web of your hand between your thumb and forefinger. Nobody knows where this story started but it is a scuba diving urban myth, repeated so frequently and so authoritatively that it has become universally acknowledged as the truth.

It is not true. Videos have been published of sea snakes wrestling with moray eels and consuming the eels headfirst. The sea snake can extend its jaws to 180 degrees, each jaw sliding sideways while the snake's skin stretches.

If you see a sea snake during a dive, watch it, marvel at its manoeuvrability and wonder at how a land-based animal has adapted itself so completely to the sea. If it approaches you, get out of the way. Don't test its patience by aggravating it and, whatever you do, don't hold your hand out to see if I am correct or if the urban myth is true after all.

Blue Ringed Octopus

The blue-ringed octopus is a true marine celebrity, famous for the potency of its venom and the fact that no anti-venom exists. It bites you; you die. What an exciting animal this must be! Sadly, like many celebrities, when you meet it, it is much smaller than you thought it would be and much more boring than you expected.

The octopus only shows its blue rings when it is provoked so, having read this far through the chapter, you can probably guess what happens when divers come along and are disappointed that it is tiny, dull and brown against a dull brown seabed. Yes, that's right, they provoke it so that it displays those famous blue rings and they manipulate it towards a more photogenic background. Normally, when threatened, the octopus will flee. It is only when cornered that it deploys its weaponry. When you see one, be amazed that this insignificant little creature is so incredibly lethal and leave it to get on with its life undisturbed.

Sea Urchins

You will rarely come across a blue–ringed octopus on a dive but you will come across sea urchins all the time. Although they cannot deliver anywhere near the punch of a "blue ring," you should nevertheless steer well clear. Sea urchin spine injuries are very common, especially on night dives when many species are more active. The spines are hard to remove completely, the wounds are very painful and they take a long time to heal.

When you look at urchins, you may find it hard to think of them as animals with brains but that is what they are. They use their spines for protection, to trap food particles and move about. The key word here is use. If you are moving close to sea urchins, you are a threat and they will deploy their spines to defend themselves.

If you have been tagged by an urchin, the normal treatment is to try to remove the whole spine, clean the puncture site and apply hydrocortisone cream. This will reduce inflammation around any bits of spine that may remain in the wound. It can take weeks for the irritation to disappear. Sea urchins are bottom dwellers so they are yet another good reason for you to work on developing good buoyancy skills and keep off the seabed.

Start diving the right way by

giving the inhabitants of the sea the respect that is their due.

22. The Scuba Safety People

It was a sunny day in French Polynesia. The two divers, John and his wife Denise, were following Francis, their guide, through an atoll pass. The current was carrying them all along at a comfortable speed through large schools of fish and, from time to time, grey reef sharks would appear out in the blue. It was exciting stuff! However, the dive was about to get more exciting and for all the wrong reasons.

Francis noticed that John seemed to have too much weight on his weightbelt. He had inflated his BCD to compensate but this just meant that he was almost vertical in the water, rather than horizontal. Francis made a mental note to advise him to remove some of the weight when they were all back on the boat after the dive. He also moved a little closer to John, to try to catch his attention and get him to reposition and tighten his weightbelt.

Francis was therefore almost perfectly placed to react when John's weightbelt came loose. Unfortunately he was not quite close enough. The belt slid down John's legs, caught briefly on his fins and then plummeted into the depths. As John headed fast for the surface, his inflated BCD expanding as he went up, Francis grabbed hold of his leg and went up with him, trying desperately to reach John's BCD dump valve to slow him down. Francis had the presence of mind to exhale continuously as John pulled him up and when they reached the surface, John was unconscious, but Francis was OK, at least for now.

Francis signalled the boat, helped the crewmen remove John's equipment and watched as they pulled John up and on to the deck. Francis looked around and saw that Denise had now surfaced too and was swimming on her back towards the boat. One crewman was waiting to help her get on board while the other was checking John's vital signs. He was still out cold but he had a pulse and was breathing.

The boat was carrying emergency oxygen. Francis was a Divers Alert Network (DAN) oxygen instructor and had trained both crewmen as oxygen providers. They set about administering oxygen to John, while the boat captain called out on the radio for an ambulance to meet them at the dock.

Francis accompanied John and Denise to hospital, continuing to administer oxygen until they arrived. When they got there, he explained to the doctor what had happened and asked if a nurse could take over oxygen duties while he called the DAN emergency hotline. He got through immediately to the DAN diving doctor on duty and, after reporting what had happened so far, he handed the phone over to the local doctor.

After speaking to DAN for a few minutes, the local doctor thanked Francis and handed back the phone. The line was still open and the DAN doctor said that it was extremely likely that John would require recompression therapy. As there was no chamber on the island, he would have to be evacuated. He asked if John and Denise were DAN members and had DAN dive accident insurance. Francis told him their insurance was current and gave him their membership numbers. The DAN doctor said they would take care of everything and asked to speak to Denise.

John and Denise both left the island that afternoon. John underwent several sessions of recompression therapy and eventually he made a full recovery.

What is DAN?

DAN is the Divers Alert Network, the largest, most important and most active organization in the world dedicated to sport diving safety. For over 30 years, DAN has; -

1. provided emergency assistance to scuba divers in trouble;

2. advised generations of divers on diving-related medical matters;

3. conducted research into how scuba divers and snorkelers come to harm;

4. campaigned on a wide range of issues to make the sport safer;

5. educated thousands of instructors in how to provide oxygen first aid;

6. worked tirelessly to promote the provision of on site oxygen in diving operations to give injured divers like John a better chance of survival; and

7. developed diving's first accident insurance programme, having recognized the need for scuba divers to have insurance to help cover the cost of treatment for scuba diving injuries.

It was research conducted by DAN that led to the establishment of the flying after diving recommendations that we currently follow. DAN also monitors both scuba diving and breath-hold diving accidents. It collects data from participants and witnesses, then compiles an annual report, which is freely available to everyone.

DAN collects dive profile information in order to conduct a statistical analysis of the risks of decompression illness (DCI). It conducts research into diver health and fitness and the question of whether people with certain conditions should be permitted to scuba dive. An important recent project initiated by DAN has been to assess how divers who have a heart condition known as patent foramen ovale (PFO) should be treated. The condition is associated with an increased risk of DCI and I referred to it earlier in the chapter "Health and Watermanship."

One of DAN's best-known resources is the 24-hour Emergency Hotline that Francis called in order to put the local doctor in touch with a specialist in diving medicine. Not many doctors anywhere in the world, never mind remote locations, are experts in diving medicine but the doctor manning the DAN Hotline certainly is.

If a you are a diver, you have an accident and someone calls the Hotline on your behalf, the doctor on duty will offer advice and recommendations whether you are a DAN member or not. This alone is a terrific testament to the organisation's standards of care and professionalism.

If you have DAN insurance coverage then DAN will take over management of the situation. If you have coverage via another insurer then this insurer must be contacted. If you have no insurance coverage or your coverage does not cover scuba diving accidents, then someone needs to be found who can pay for treatment and evacuation, if necessary. This can be extremely expensive. Many dive operations make sure that everyone who wants to dive with them has current diving accident insurance. If you don't, then operations can often help you arrange it on the spot, but it is best not to rely on this.

DAN also provides divers with a number of non-emergency resources, including the DAN Information Line, medical FAQs, online seminars and the Alert Diver Magazine. The organisation is a non-profit and entirely funded by grants, donations, membership dues and insurance sales. By becoming a DAN member and buying DAN insurance, not only do you protect yourself if you are ever the victim of a diving accident, you also keep up to date on research into diving safety and you contribute to the well-being of the diving community at large.

A Personal Note

I have been a DAN member for 25 years or so and, when I was teaching, I was a DAN Oxygen Instructor Trainer. This chapter may come over as something of a sales pitch, which I suppose it is, in a way. Rest assured, however, that nobody has asked me or paid me to write it, nor do I gain in any way by promoting DAN and its services. Most courses for beginners tend not to tell new divers what DAN is and the great things it does. These are omissions I wanted to correct.

Start diving the right way by

becoming a DAN member.

23. It Happened to Me

While I was writing Scuba Fundamental, I wrote and asked a few friends, all now experienced divers, to send me stories of things that happened to them when they first learned to dive.

I have used some of the tales to illustrate earlier chapters in the book but I thought you might like to read some more, so I added this extra chapter. All of these are true stories, even the ones that may seem incredible. None of the names have been changed!

Bart

For the open water dives on our beginner's course, our instructor took me and my group to a quarry in the south of Belgium. The highlight of my first dive on scuba was seeing my first fish underwater! The second dive, one week later, was more challenging. On this dive I had to share air with another diver.

At a depth of around 10m (33 ft), my instructor, who was facing me, indicated that I should tell him I was out of air by slicing my hand back and forth in front of my throat. He then removed his regulator from his mouth and gave it to me. I put it in my mouth, exhaled to clear the water out and started breathing from it. Meanwhile, my instructor switched to his octopus regulator.

After a minute or so, he indicated that the drill was over. I returned his regulator to him and started breathing from my own.

My instructor then gave me the signal that this time it was he who was 'out of air.' Now it was my turn to impress. Without hesitation, I took my regulator out of my mouth and handed it over. I then reached for my octopus regulator. At that time, I was using something called an Air2. This was a regulator integrated into my BCD inflator hose, so it was located just below my left shoulder. What followed was rather scary.

I grabbed the mouthpiece with my left hand, exhaled briefly to clear it and then inhaled gently. I tasted water, so I exhaled again and inhaled more forcefully. I needed air by this time! Unfortunately, I didn't get any air. Instead, all I got was a mouthful of quarry water. I choked, tore my regulator back out of the instructor's mouth, (too bad for him,) and spent the next minute or two trying to calm down. I could see from the look in my instructor's eyes and the constant stream of bubbles he was producing that this was evidently one of the funniest things he had ever seen. It didn't seem funny to me.

As I later discovered, instead of taking my Air2 to breathe from, I had grabbed my snorkel instead and tried to breathe from that. At a depth of 10m (33ft) that was never going to work! In my defence, I was wearing thick gloves because the water in this Belgian quarry was cold, so I could not really feel the difference. Of course, I was the butt of jokes for the rest of the course. Actually, I was quite proud of myself, not because I had done a stupid thing but because I had not panicked and shot to the surface. I had technically killed my instructor but, hey, that is why he gets paid the big bucks!

Cindy

Having dived a lot in warm water in Southeast Asia, I returned to Western Australia and, while I was there, I decided to do my Advanced Course. In terms of number of dives logged, I was the most experienced student in the group and, I admit, I had been telling a few "war stories" about all the dives I had done. The first dive on the course was to take place at a site called the Rockingham Wreck Trail, a shore dive next to a busy road.

As I would be diving in colder water, I had bought a 7mm wetsuit and would be wearing it for the first time. It took me an age to get it on and, seeing me struggling with it, drivers passing by would honk their horn and wind their window down to shout encouragement. At least, that was what I hoped they were shouting. The rest of the group went into the water ahead of me and waited at the buoy marking the descent line.

Finally, I managed to get my suit and dive gear on. I shuffled across the beach, entered the water, put my fins on and finned backwards on the surface towards the group. After a while, I turned and saw that I had almost reached them. The instructor caught my eye and gave me the OK signal, which I returned. Evidently impatient at the delay and rightly worried that the other divers had already been hanging around in the cool water for quite some time, he gave them the signal to begin the dive and they all descended.

I eventually arrived at the buoy, exhausted and very stressed. The group had gone but the jacuzzi of their bubbles was all around me. I knew where they were. I knew I should wait and get my breath back before starting my dive but I felt bad at having made them wait so long already. So I immediately deflated my BCD, exhaled and dropped down into what could best be described as an ocean of milk.

All the dives I had ever done had been in clear, warm water. Here, I couldn't see a thing. I was still breathing hard from my exertions and I felt a rising tide of anxiety as I looked for the seabed. I found it when I crashed into it and managed to lose the regulator from my mouth at the same time. Reaching to recover it, I somehow managed to crack my head against a hard metal object, which, I later found out, was a light aircraft – exhibit number one on the Wreck Trail.

My head was ringing; my chest was heaving: my mind was shot through with stress. I had had enough. Up I went, remembering to breathe as I ascended. I went back to the beach, changed, packed everything into the car and drove off, leaving a note under the instructor's windscreen wiper, saying "sorry, emergency, had to go." I remember being very relieved that I had managed to avoid facing the group and having to admit my failings. Later, after I had managed to come up with what I thought might be an acceptable excuse, I called the instructor and apologised for deserting him.

He told me that, when I failed to appear underwater, he had assembled the group and they had all surfaced just in time to see me scooting up the beach as fast as my wetsuited legs could carry me. So he knew I was OK. He said he hoped I would come back and do the advanced course at a later date, suggesting tactfully that I do a few easy, shallow, local dives in the meantime, to acclimatise myself to more temperate waters. And that was what I did. A couple of months later, I tried again and it all went perfectly.

Garry

While I was backpacking around Greece in 2001, I stopped off to visit a friend in Cyprus who was doing a Rescue Diver course. Late on the first afternoon, I wandered over while the group was gathered on the beach and the instructor asked if I was a diver. I had only just completed my initial course but I proudly told him that yes, I was a diver, without elaborating on my level of experience. He asked if I could help by acting as a victim on the next dive. I agreed and asked what I should do. "Grab some equipment, then swim over there, find a big rock or something and hide behind it. The students will conduct a search and, when they find you, they will bring you to the surface, take you back to the shore and administer CPR."

So, while they were all getting ready to go into the water, off I went, found a large rock in a depth of about 7m (23ft) and lay behind it. After 30 minutes or so, (I had my cool, new diver's watch on,) I thought, "hmm, they should have found me by now." Another 20 minutes passed. It was now dark and I was getting cold. I looked around but I couldn't see any lights. Alarm bells started going off in my head but I didn't want to let the instructor down, so I just stayed there.

A few minutes later, I glanced down at my contents gauge, not really thinking that I would be low on air, as I was only shallow and had not been moving about much. I was just bored. But when I saw that I had only 10Bar (150psi) left in my cylinder, that woke me up and I decided to get out of there in a hurry. At the surface, the stars were out but there was no sign of any divers. So I swam back to the shore. I walked up the beach, through the hotel's ornate gardens, climbed up the stone steps to the bar, still in my gear, and there they all were, drinking coffee. They asked where I had been and said they hadn't been able to find me so had just given up. There was no apology. They didn't even offer to buy me a coffee!

Jim

It was a stormy day in Idaho and it was the last dive of my beginner's class. Our instructor had told my buddy and me to execute an emergency ascent together. We were to simulate that we had run out of air, with no other option but to swim to the surface slowly, with the deflate button on our BCD open and continuously exhaling.

Somehow, although my buddy and I got everything else right, we apparently missed the word "slowly" in the instructions and our ascent became more of a race. We broke the surface with a splash and were shouting with excitement, both claiming victory. Our instructor arrived moments later and he started shouting too, but he was shouting at us for being so incredibly stupid. Looking back, I can't believe what a foolish thing we did, coming up so fast, but we were not much more than kids. It was playtime.

The instructor was obviously scared that we might have come to harm and that is why he was so upset, but when he stopped screaming, we all heard someone else shouting at us from the shore. It was the instructor's assistant. We originally thought that he was just angry at our behaviour too, but, when we all swam over, he explained that, while we had all been underwater, the pond had been struck by lightning. He thought we might have all been fried and was ecstatic to see us all alive! Thinking back, I remembered feeling a tingle at one point during the dive and making a mental note to ask the instructor about it later.

Kim

I was on a navigation dive in Guam with four or five other divers. We had finished our navigation exercises in the sand and were heading back to the shallows when, all of a sudden, a rogue wave broke over us. Visibility dropped to nothing immediately and the wave picked us up and tumbled us head over fins the whole way to the beach. We were all separated. We stood up and then got knocked over again by a series of further waves until finally the sea retreated. I stood up and looked around. Everyone was lying shocked and stranded on the rocks and sand that had just a few seconds ago been covered in several feet of water.

I did a quick head count. Nobody was missing. We all crawled further up the beach, gathered together and exchanged stories. Nobody had panicked. Nobody had even lost a mask or any other equipment. Those without wetsuits just had a few cuts and scrapes. Although each of us was scared while it was happening, we just kept breathing and waited until it all stopped. We didn't have time to think about doing anything else. That night we heard that an undersea earthquake had been reported around the same time we were in the water. All I can think is that what we experienced was a consequence of that: some sort of mini-tsunami.

Mike

Early on in my diving life, I was out on a boat with a group of eight divers. My buddy and I were down about an hour and surfaced at the exact buoy where the boat had been tied up when we descended. But the boat had gone. We stayed on the surface and didn't move. About 20 minutes later, a boat from another dive centre showed up. They took us on board and we hung out with the crew while the new group went diving. When we returned to the dive centre we had originally gone out with to return our cylinders and weights, they just said "sorry Man!" We got the impression that this sort of thing happened all the time. I decided I would do more research and choose my dive operation more carefully in future.

A few years later, I went diving again, this time on Guam. The boat anchored in a distinctively shaped shallow, sandy area. My buddy and I just swam around the reef and had a great time. We returned to the sand patch a little earlier than planned, but arrived just as our boat left! We could see the disturbance in the sand where the anchor had been and we heard the engine roar as it took off. "Not again!" I thought.

Some more divers showed up. We all had plenty of air left and one of the divers indicated that we should just stay in the area of the sand flat for a while, instead of surfacing. After about 15 minutes, we heard a vessel above us and we all ascended. It was our boat. The crew explained that they had seen some divers drifting and signalling for help further down the coast and had gone to pick them up. There were two of them, sitting huddled in towels on the deck. They had been diving from a beach, got caught in an offshore current and had been unable to get back to shore. Having picked them up, our boat then returned for us as quickly as possible. The captain apologised for any distress we might have been caused but he hoped we understood the decision he had made. Of course we did. I dived a lot more with that dive centre during my time on Guam.

Peter

Shortly after getting certified, I was lucky enough to go diving in the Galapagos Islands. It was the end of the dive, everyone else was back in the tender boat and I was finishing my safety stop, when I saw a school of eagle rays sweep past me, swimming faster than I ever thought rays could swim. I didn't even have time to speculate what would make a school of rays move that quickly when the first killer whale swam by, followed by a second and then by the rest of the pod. What a thrill! They soon disappeared into the murk and I made my ascent. The tender boat and all my companions had shot off after the orcas, leaving me behind, but I had so much adrenaline coursing through my bloodstream that I didn't care. When they came back for me, I was lying on my back, being massaged by the rolling waves and humming "What a Wonderful World!" to myself.

Tracy

Dateline: Late March and April 1997.

Weeks 1 through 3: Open Water certification: Thursday evening pool sessions: discomfort and anxiety due to mask leak and a too-tight 7mm suit.

Week 4: Open Water certification: four checkout dives in Monterey, 10C (50F) water and I thought I saw a starfish.

Week 5: fly to Australia on business: take a weekend trip to Heron Island. It is my first dive as a certified diver. One minute into the dive, I am 6m (20ft) below the surface and I look up as a 4m (12ft) manta ray swims above me.

I decide at that point that I will be a diver for the rest of my life.

Acknowledgements

I am indebted to a number of people for giving me the inspiration to write Scuba Fundamental, for sharing their stories with me or for listening patiently while I bounced ideas off them.

First of all, my wife Sofie, who is responsible for the whole idea of Scuba Fundamental and for so much else besides.

I am grateful to story contributors Bart Adams, David Strike, Garry Hudson, Jeff O'Halloran, Peter Van Scoik, Tracy Grogan, Kim and Mike Smith, Mandy Gurr, Jim Pinson, Cindy Egan, Marna Cahn, Kerri Bingham, Andrina Bindon, Simon Marsh, Jan Brown and Anne K. Adijuwono. You provided many of this book's WOW moments.

Thanks especially to Hergen Spalink for the excellent idea of including a chapter on underwater photography in Scuba Fundamental. Hergen is a world-class underwater photographer. I am not. Any technical inaccuracies in the chapter are my fault, certainly not his.

Spaseeba again to Andrey Bizyukin for another great cover image and much gratitude to John Lippman for his valuable input.

Finally I would like to record my appreciation for the work of the fine folk at Createspace, Amazon and ACX. I could not have chosen better publishing partners.

About the Author

Simon Pridmore was born in England and brought up around the world. After spells as a teacher in Algeria and Oman, he joined the Royal Hong Kong Police in 1982. Ten years later he transferred to the Hong Kong Civil Service, an experience he credits with developing his writing skills. He left Hong Kong in 1997 to become a full-time dive professional and has never looked back.

Simon learned to dive in Oman in 1981. He trained with the Sultan's Armed Forces BSAC Dive Club and was drafted by the club to help teach classes almost immediately after graduation as a Class 3 diver because he was a "schoolie." Later he joined PADI as an Instructor then trained with Rob Cason at Fun Dive in Sydney, Australia to become one of the first technical diving instructor trainers in Asia.

In 1995, in Phuket, Thailand, Simon helped Rob run the first NITROX instructor trainer course in Asia. Later the same year, he and Paul Neilsen of Mandarin Divers in Hong Kong taught one of the first Advanced NITROX Instructor Courses in the region. The course was conducted simultaneously at La Laguna Beach Resort and Captain Greggs in Puerto Galera in the Philippines and among the students was future world depth record holder John Bennett.

In 1996 Simon participated in the first sport rebreather training course in Asia, using ex-Australian Navy Dräger FGTs. He then completed cave diver and TRIMIX Diver training with Tom Mount in Florida, USA. In 1997, he established Professional Sports Divers in Guam, the first dedicated technical diver training centre in the Asia-Pacific and assisted Tom Mount in Thailand with the first TRIMIX Instructor Course in Asia.

The same year, Simon dived with Capt. Billy Deans when he was contracted to carry out deep-water surveys using TRIMIX of the suspected wreck site of the sunken Spanish galleon Nuestra Senora del Pilar off the southern tip of Guam. In 2001, he was part of Kevin Gurr's Pilar Project team, which conducted what was, at the time, the most extensive operation ever attempted by sport divers exclusively on closed circuit rebreathers.

Between 1997 and 2003 Simon was licensee of the Micronesia franchise of IANTD, which included facilities in Palau, Truk, Kosrae, Majuro and Bikini. Then from 2003 to 2008 he owned and ran the IANTD franchise in the United Kingdom. While in the UK he also worked as Head of Sales, Marketing & Technical Support for Delta P Technology and Closed Circuit Research Ltd: manufacturers of the Ouroboros and Sentinel Closed Circuit Rebreathers and the VR range of dive computers.

Today Simon lives, writes and dives in Bali, Indonesia. As well as *Scuba Fundamental* and its companion volumes in the series, *Scuba Confidential, Scuba Exceptional, Scuba Professional* and *Scuba Physiological*, he has written hundreds of articles and features on diver training and travel for magazines including Diver, Sport Diver, Asian Diver, Action Asia, EZDive, X Ray, Dive Log and Asian Geographic. Simon is also the co- author, with Tim Rock, of a number of diving and snorkelling guides to Indonesia and, with David Strike, of a unique storybook – cookbook series called *Dining with Divers*. Away from scuba diving, he has also published a travelogue called *Under the Flight Path*. Find out more about Simon and his books at www.simonpridmore.com.

Also by Simon Pridmore

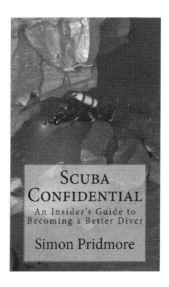

Scuba Confidential - An Insider's Guide to Becoming a Better Diver (Sandsmedia 2013)

Scuba Exceptional – Become the Best Diver You Can Be (Sandsmedia 2018)

Scuba Professional – Insights into Sport Diver Training & Operations (Sandsmedia 2015)

Scuba Physiological – Think You Know All About Scuba Medicine? Think Again! (Sandsmedia 2017)

Dining with Divers – Tales from the Kitchen Table (Sandsmedia 2017)

Dining with Divers – A Taste for Adventure (Sandsmedia 2018)

Praise for Simon Pridmore's Scuba Confidential

"If PADI's Open-Water manual is the Bible of scuba diving, consider this the New Testament. Scuba Confidential is the closest thing there is to a scuba diving self-help book and a must-read for any diver, new or old." **David Espinosa, Editor in Chief, Sport Diver magazines**

"Instead of writing another training manual, Simon has utilised a very unique approach to sharing his many years of experience underwater with those that may be thinking of becoming a diver or are already enjoying the wonders of the underwater world. Through the use of case histories Simon provides a black-box approach to avoiding some of diving's pitfalls and in doing so, he gives some great tips and insights on subjects important to divers at all levels that may not be found in other publications." **Terry Cummins OMA**

"Packed full of thoughtful – and thought-provoking – information, tips, analyses and insights gleaned from more than thirty years as a widely-respected diving industry professional, Simon Pridmore's, 'Scuba Confidential: An Insider's Guide To Becoming A Better Diver', is required reading for all divers, regardless of experience level, whose minds remain open to the book's underlying message that, "Learning to dive is easy; becoming a good diver is hard." 'Scuba Confidential' is much more than just another, 'How-To' diving manual." **David Strike, OZTeK Organiser**

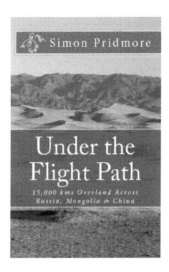

Under the Flight Path: 15,000 kms Overland Across Russia, Mongolia & China (Sandsmedia / Createspace 2017)

"A vivid, witty account of a couple's no-frills travel across Eurasia. An inspiration to real travellers - Yes! It's Possible! Do it! - but also an entertainment for those who prefer their armchairs." **John Man, author of Genghis Khan, Life, Death and Resurrection**

"Entertaining and informative, written in a lively, engaging style and the narrative flows beautifully." **Jackie Winter, author of Life in Tandem and Lipsticks and Library Books**

"Under the Flight Path is a special travel memoir that is a journey in itself. Warm, candid and funny." **Amy Johnstone, author and founder of Story**

"A fast-paced page-turner featuring Simon's special brand of humour, insight and knowledge of Russian and Asian culture and history. What a delight! **Tim Rock, Lonely Planet author**

Finally, do you listen to audiobooks? Would you like to give them a try?

Some of Simon Pridmore's books are available as audiobooks too. These include: -

Scuba Fundamental – Start Diving the Right Way

Scuba Confidential – An Insider's Guide to Becoming a Better Diver

Scuba Professional – Insights into Sport Diver Training & Operations

Secretos De Buceo: La Guia del Conocedor para Transformarte en un Mejor Buzo (Scuba Confidential in Spanish)

Under the Flight Path: 15,000 kms Overland Across Russia, Mongolia & China

More information can be found at
www.simonpridmore.com

Made in the USA
Middletown, DE
10 May 2019